To Walk Humbly

Stories and Activities for Teaching Compassion and Justice
for Ages Ten through Thirteen

You have already been told what is right and what Yahweh wants of you.
Only this, to act justly, to love tenderly, and to walk humbly with your God.

• Micah 6:8

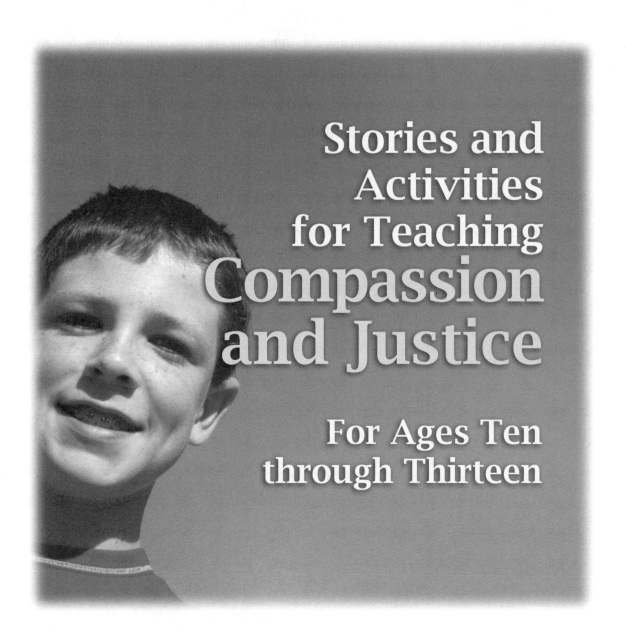

Stories and Activities for Teaching Compassion and Justice

For Ages Ten through Thirteen

ANNE E. NEUBERGER

TWENTY
THIRD 23rd
PUBLICATIONS

Dedication

For the world's children: may they grow up healthy, strong, and well-educated, and may they grow together in compassion and appreciation.

Acknowledgments

The author thanks those who helped bring this book about: Joyana Jacoby, Donald H. Dunson, Jeffrey Griffith, Danielle Funk, Paul Ismail, Anna and Silvija Kancans, Diane Nunnelee, Fr. Mike Schwarte, Rick Cousins, Lisa Amman, Joe Towalski, Greg Auberry, Andrew Wells-Dang, Kathryn Runman-Zimney, Amy Ellingson, Anne Attea, Martin Hartney, Jacqueline DeCarlo, and Abi Thatcher. Also, thanks to those who helped test out the activity materials: Patti Cibuzar and her 2005–06 fifth grade class, and her 2004–05 fifth grade class; Kelli Kester and her confirmation class, Doran Schrantz, Chris Conry, and Paul Marincel.

Twenty-Third Publications
A Division of Bayard
One Montauk Avenue, Suite 200
New London, CT 06320
(860) 437-3012 or (800) 321-0411
www.23rdpublications.com

ISBN 978-1-58595-616-6
Library of Congress Catalog Card Number: 2006937992
Printed in the U.S.A.

Contents

Introduction

In each century, our world has been a place of conflict and war, of starvation in the midst of plenty, of riches gained by some by depriving others. It was that way when Jesus walked on earth, and it is that way today.

However, in every era, there is also a strong force for the good and the just. Jesus, the Light of the world, is our best example. Over the centuries since Jesus' death and resurrection, there have always been people who followed his teachings to bring the light of love, fairness, and compassion to a suffering world. Indeed, in looking back at history, we can see that at many times, the only hope was this love and compassion that good Christians and other caring people brought about.

In each generation, Christians are called by Jesus to spread hope through compassion and to work for justice for those who are treated unfairly. When we baptize our children, we pass on this heritage and are responsible for guiding and teaching our children to act on this heritage. The need for this is perhaps more urgent in this generation than for earlier ones. Today's global economy, touching people in even the most remote regions of the world, brings the threat of rampant injustice. The staggering number of children forced to work in one country to produce goods for people in other countries is one example. Other issues, such as pollution and the abuse of natural resources are impacting the populations in many areas. The need for compassion and social justice, as well as preparing our children to work for social justice, has become essential. We need to give them the tools to answer Jesus' call to build the kingdom. Indeed, to raise children to act on compassion, justice, and fairness is our greatest hope.

Using this Book

Part One: The Stories

To develop a sense of compassion and justice in learners, this book uses one of our strongest, most ancient, and perhaps most delightful tools for passing on wisdom and information: stories. Through stories of children in various parts of the world, living in a variety of economic, cultural, and political conditions, learners will become more aware of their peers in the greater world. They will learn of situations and settings they would be unlikely to find described in other books. The purpose of the stories is to help learners develop a strong sense of identity with other children as their brothers and sisters. This identification will hopefully develop in them compassion, empathy, and a desire to work against the injustices that many of their sisters and brothers suffer.

We recommend that the group leader—whether catechist, teacher, youth minister, or parent—read these stories aloud to their learners, even when the learners are able to read the stories themselves (there are a few exceptions when reading parts are indicated for the learners). People always benefit from listening to a story, no matter what their ages and abilities. Following a story by listening exercises a different kind of brain function than reading does. Listening also enriches the learners' appreciation for language. Most importantly, sharing a story with others through group reading can be a powerful experience, the kind that leads to new ways of viewing the world and identifying with others. These stories may also be quite different from topics the learners are accustomed to, and the group leader can help facilitate discussions.

The stories can be used by themselves. A story that has its own effect on a person is always powerful.

Preceding each story are Directions and an Introduction. The Directions contain extra background for the leader, as well as activities that can be used to introduce, reinforce, or review the story. The Introduction sets the mood and location and offers information about each story. Before beginning the story the leader may share this material with the listeners. The stories are also applied in many different ways in Parts Two and Three.

Before reading each story, the leader and group may locate the country or countries mentioned in it on a map or globe. Mark the countries on a map. As the learners progress with the stories, they can see where certain countries are in relation to others. This will enhance their sense of world geography and assist them in developing a global outlook and a sense of solidarity.

No social justice issue is particularly pleasant, so all the stories are written with the maturity levels and ages of the listeners taken into consideration. However, it is also important for adults to keep in mind that stories we may shy away from telling our children are the actual situations many of their peers live with daily.

As catechists, teachers, and parents, you will find hope in many of these stories. Your learners will understand that great possibilities exist, born out of compassion and creativity, and these can lead to tremendous and positive change. This fact may give them the courage to become part of the solution.

Part Two: Introducing Catholic Social Teaching

This section presents a very brief history of the Catholic Church and social justice. It explains what are commonly referred to as the "principles of Catholic social teaching," in a language accessible to learners ages ten through thirteen. It also suggests how to use the stories to connect the principles with real life.

Part Three: Learning and Teaching

Part Three features activities that will greatly advance the learners' knowledge about two of the topics found in the stories: hunger and child labor. It also includes creative ways for learners to use that knowledge to teach others. For example, they will be able to set up displays and present information in their church communities and schools so they can share what they've studied with adults and other children of various ages. This project reinforces the concepts and also empowers the learners, giving them the tools and the confidence to be socially responsible Catholics. Although not every parish or school will have the time or materials for an exhibit, the activities that form the project may be done individually.

Of course, much work needs to be done if we are to make real and substantial changes related to the issues addressed in this book. Children can be effective in this work. The scope of *To Walk Humbly* is to awake and motivate the abilities of children by nurturing a world view and an awareness of injustice and to give learners the confidence to become voices for justice. Suggestions for ways to become further involved are listed throughout Part Three.

My personal hope is that these stories and activities will give young people an opportunity to experience a sense of solidarity with other children in the world. May God bless you and your learners as together you "live justly, love tenderly, and walk humbly with your God."

A.E.N.

Part One

The Stories

The purpose of the work, be it story, music, or painting,
is to further the coming of the kingdom,
to make us aware of our status of children of God.

• Madeleine L'Engle

One Hundred Welcomes

A Story from Iraq

DIRECTIONS: Talk about what learners know about Iraq and the Iraqi people before reading the story. After reading it, discuss what they learned. Did the story add to what they already knew or contradict what they thought? Speculate what other information the group is missing about the Iraqi people. Ask if any learners would be interested in doing further research to learn more about the lives of families and children in Iraq.

INTRODUCTION: In 2002, before the second Gulf War, an American woman, Lisa Amman, visited Iraq. She found a culture where hospitality is extremely important. Though families sometimes did not have enough food for themselves, they would offer what they had to guests. The Iraqi people she met were open and friendly. They were interested in others and ready to make friends, even when they did not speak the same language.

Lisa Amman approached the little concrete block house. She had accepted an invitation to visit a local family as she traveled in Iraq. Though the day was extremely hot, about 130 degrees Fahrenheit, she could not turn them down just because of the high temperature.

She was ushered into the house where several small children, older children, grandparents, uncles, and parents greeted her happily.

Lisa felt stifled by the heat in the house, but took the seat offered her on a mat that lay along the walls of the main room. She was given a sweet tea made with dried lemons. Lisa was grateful but wondered if she could first wash her hands. She had been traveling all day in the heat and dust. She made her request using gestures.

One of the women nodded and led her into the kitchen. An eight-year-old girl followed them. Lisa saw a bucket of water and a wash basin. The woman took Lisa's hands in hers to show her that she was to hold them over the basin. The girl then carefully poured enough water over Lisa's hands to wet them thoroughly and she handed Lisa a piece of soap. The child stood quietly nearby as Lisa lathered her hands, but smiled whenever Lisa glanced at her. When the girl saw that Lisa had finished, she poured more water over Lisa's hands to rinse off the soap.

Lisa felt honored by this act of kindness and attentiveness. It reminded her of Jesus washing the feet of his apostles.

Back with the rest of the group, Lisa delighted in the antics of the toddlers who did silly dances, clapped their hands, and jumped around the room. The adults in the family enjoyed the show, too, but seemed concerned about something else.

With some difficulty and much shared laughter over the language differences, they were able to tell their guest that the family had limited access to electricity but had saved it for this visit.

"We intended to put on our fan while you were here," Lisa was able to understand, "but now the fan doesn't work. We are so very sorry not to have a fan on!"

As soon as they had communicated their regret, the girl who helped Lisa earlier and her older brother approached Lisa. They had towels in hand and began fanning her with the towels. No one had told them to do this, but they seemed glad to help.

All this time, one little girl had watched everything quietly, not joining her younger brother and cousins in their baby antics. Then she, too, found a way to welcome the guest. Lisa felt a tap on her shoulder. She turned and looked into the shining dark eyes of the little girl, who then said softly in English, "One, two, three, four...."

Lisa smiled and congratulated her on this accomplishment. When the child reached the number ten, the little one smiled back and added, "Eleven, twelve, thirteen...."

Lisa clapped again at twenty. "Twenty-one, twenty-two...."

This gracious welcome continued until the girl had counted to one hundred. Lisa realized that the welcome of this family knew no bounds.

Tiny Knots and Heavy Chains

A Story from India

DIRECTIONS: Using the principles of Catholic social teaching (see page 101), examine the circumstances of Ramatha's life. What was he missing? What did he need? This story can be acted out as it has many physical actions.

INTRODUCTION: Child labor takes on many forms. Carpet-making factories using children is one area that has received much attention. Due to the publicity, many children have been freed. In India and Pakistan, famous for their carpets, severe poverty forces parents and children into exploitive situations. Rugmark is a global, non-profit organization working to end illegal child labor. It also offers educational opportunities to children in India, Nepal, and Pakistan. For more information, go to **www.rugmark.org**.

Ramatha sat at the loom, tying tiny knots. The rug he was creating was intricate and beautiful. Someone would pay a great deal of money for it.

Ramatha would never see any of that money.

His eyes hurt from working in the dimly-lit factory. His fingers ached from hours and hours of knot tying. His head throbbed from lack of food. His legs were cramped from sitting all day.

After several more hours and a small amount of food, Ramatha would lay down next to the loom to sleep on the dirt floor. He was eight years old, and his life was spent here, seven days a week.

Many other boys also worked at the looms. Recently one of the bigger boys had tried to escape the factory. He was caught, beaten badly, and brought back to work. From then on, he was chained to his loom. So Ramatha never thought of trying to escape.

He did think about home.

Home was a tiny place made of mud-brick walls. His village had no electricity or running water. Everyone was desperately poor.

One day, a well-dressed man from a city had come to the village. Curious, some of the village people had greeted him. He spoke to them with great courtesy. "I've come to help you. I want to teach your boys a good skill. If you'll let them come with me, I'll teach them to be carpet makers. When they're grown, they will be able to get good jobs!" the man had promised. "For a few hours each day, your boys will be taught how to make carpets. Then they'll go to school. I'll give them their meals and a place to sleep. The money they earn by making carpets will be sent home to you."

The parents were so poor they could hardly feed their children. This was the answer to many of their problems! So Ramatha and other village boys had been allowed to go with this man to his factory. He took them so far from home that they did not know how to get back.

That was a long time ago. Now, hungry and homesick, Ramatha tried to sleep.

The next morning Ramatha and the other boys were working as usual when the door burst open. Police and other people rushed into the factory. "You're free now," one of the police officers shouted. "You can go home!"

Ramatha was stunned. Was this a trick? But no, a police officer was unlocking the chains from a boy's leg.

He heard one of the adults say that the factory owner was being arrested.

Dirty, hungry, and bewildered, Ramatha and the other boys blinked in the bright sunshine as they were led outside. A jeep was waiting. The adults asked many questions, trying to find out where the boys' village was located. Meanwhile they gave the boys food and water.

Ramatha breathed the fresh air. He tasted the delicious food. But it wasn't until he was on the jeep that he really understood that he was going home. The rest of the day and all night long they rode over bumpy roads. Before the sun was up, they arrived at Ramatha's village.

Everyone there was sleeping, but the people woke at the sound of the jeep. The families heard the boys shouting, "We're home! We're free!"

People came running from all directions. Ramatha searched the familiar faces for his parents.

"Ramatha?" He heard his mother's hopeful voice.

"There he is!" cried his father. They hugged and cried and hugged some more. His parents would never, ever let anyone take him again.

Ramatha's mother said, "We didn't know where you had been taken! We were so worried! You're so thin! And so dirty!"

Ramatha smiled and said, "But I'm home now, and I'm free!"

Life from Two Perspectives

A Story from the Ukraine

DIRECTIONS: The following story is based on a true incident. It is about four teenage girls, accustomed to scarcity in a Ukrainian orphanage, who are given an evening of abundance. The story offers readers an opportunity to ponder on what they have and what they take for granted. Before reading the story, locate the Ukraine on a globe or map. After reading the story, have the learners individually write comparisons of their experiences with that of the girls in the story, or a reflection on how they view their own lives.

Christina's perspective

Christina and her friends Marina, Vika, and Nadia could not believe their luck. A social worker, visiting from the United States, had offered to host a sleepover party! They were going to a real hotel. All four girls were fifteen and had grown up in orphanages. None of them had ever been to a hotel. Rebecca, the social worker, said they would enjoy food and watch a video. Christina wondered if there would be a bathtub in the room. She had never taken a bath. Perhaps she could tonight!

Rebecca's perspective

The American social worker had come to the Ukraine to visit orphanages. This was the first time she had traveled to Eastern Europe and she was delighted to meet all the wonderful young people. But the orphanages themselves left her feeling disheartened. She saw old, run-down buildings with inside walls painted a dismal pink. No pictures or posters broke the monotony. Often the water did not turn on, and the toilets did not always work. She felt sad for the children who had no choice but to grow up there.

The lack of options in their lives struck her the most. Unlike many American children, these children had no choice about the kinds or even the amount of food, though they had an adequate diet. Each child was assigned a bed, two children to a bed for those under thirteen. They could not even select their own clean pair of underwear, for there were only enough for each child to have one pair!

The children did find a way to make a selection in clothing, though the choices were limited. They traded clothes back and forth. That way they did not have to wear the same thing every day. However, the clothing did not usually fit very well and was frequently dirty.

Rebecca knew she couldn't change all this, but she could offer some girls the chance to have a different experience for one day. The orphanage director agreed, so the party was on. Rebecca was looking forward to it, but was she setting the girls up for dissatisfaction with their everyday world?

Christina's perspective

Marina, Vika, and Nadia were pointing and exclaiming over everything, beginning with the hotel lobby. Christina remained quiet, just looking and trying to remember everything. Rebecca unlocked the door to her room and the girls burst in. Marina and Nadia laughed and sank down on the large bed, and Vika headed for the television set. Christina went into the bathroom. There it was: the bathtub. It was huge! On the counter in the bathroom were Rebecca's shampoo and conditioner in large bottles. Christina wanted to get into the gigantic tub!

Since Rebecca didn't speak Ukrainian, Christina gestured toward the tub. Rebecca came into the bathroom, nodded, and turned on the faucet. Not wanting to waste any water, Christina quickly closed the drain.

To Christina's surprise, Rebecca leaned over and opened the drain and the precious water drained out! Rebecca stuck her hand under the flow of water a couple of times and when it seemed to satisfy her, closed the drain so the tub could now fill. Why had Rebecca done that?

Marina joined them. She planned to get into the tub, too. Again Rebecca said something but as neither girl understood, Rebecca handed them the shampoo and conditioner bottles. Christina looked at Marina. How much could they use?

By this time the tub was partially full, and Rebecca left the bathroom.

Christina looked at Marina and they squealed with glee. Full of joy, they both got into the tub.

"It's so warm!" Christina said. "And there is so much water! I've never seen this much water for washing before!"

Rebecca's perspective

The American woman settled into a chair as Vika and Nadia flipped through the television channels, laughing and chattering. Rebecca wasn't sure what had surprised her more: that Christina did not realize she should wait until the water was warm, or that she and Marina thought they had to use the bath at the same time to save water. Rebecca had tried to tell them they could each have a turn, but she could not make herself understood. The girls did not seem bothered that they were bathing in the same water.

Now Nadia and Vika were admiring the thick pillows and blankets, and Rebecca listened to the laughter and splashing coming from the bathroom. Eventually the door opened and Christina, wrapped in towels, came out to ask Rebecca something. Rebecca realized she was asking permission to use more shampoo. "Yes, go ahead!" Rebecca said with words and gestures.

That set the tone for the whole evening as the girls took turns, in twos, taking bath after bath after bath. They shampooed and conditioned their hair until there was nothing left in either bottle. Rebecca delighted in the raucous laughter and shrieks that came from the bathroom. She knew their tremendous pleasure came from the fact that they usually had little water or shampoo. At the orphanage, each child had a tub about the size of a dishpan, which was used for bathing, washing out clothing, and washing hair. Unlimited soap, shampoo, and bath water were a luxury. The bathtub, she guessed, must seem like an ocean.

Now it was perfume time. Rebecca had two kinds with her and she handed them over to the girls. Within seconds, they had sprayed it on themselves, each other, and their clothing. The smells of the shampoo and conditioner were almost masked by the powerful scents of the two different perfumes.

Christina's perspective

Her hair had never been so clean! Her skin had never felt so soft! She had never, ever smelled so good in her whole life! Christina closed her eyes and enjoyed the wonder of it all. When she opened them, Rebecca had started a video and was setting out food. Nadia, Marina, and Vika were exclaiming over the crackers and oranges.

Christina reached for a cracker and smiled at Rebecca. It was delicious! When she had swallowed the last of it, she looked at the plate where many crackers still remained. She looked to Rebecca, hoping she could have another. Rebecca understood and passed her the plate. The second cracker was as good as the first! Nadia held out a second orange and Rebecca gestured for her to have seconds, too. Then they all settled down to watch the video.

Rebecca's perspective

The girls asked permission for everything. They did not just sit and snack but politely asked for more. Now they were intently watching the video, even though it was in English and none of them could understand what was being said. They were so easily satisfied.

Rebecca was delighted to give the girls these pleasures for one day. She remembered how important cleanliness and good grooming had been to her when she was fifteen. Her heart ached at the thought that these girls should be deprived of water and soap and clean clothing. There was one more thing she could do, something they could keep for the dreary days ahead. She brought out the bracelets she had bought for each one. They weren't expensive, but they were pretty. She handed a little box to each girl.

Christina's perspective

Vika opened her box, which contained a lovely yellow and orange bracelet. Excited, Christina opened hers and found a bracelet also, but hers was blue and purple—her favorite colors! She jumped up, ran over to Rebecca, and threw her arms around her. "Thank you, thank you, thank you!" she said in Ukrainian, but Rebecca under-stood perfectly. Christina looked up into Rebecca's eyes and saw tears. Then she felt tears on her own cheeks, too.

Rebecca's perspective

After the baths and perfumes, the movie and food, the gifts and much more laughter, the girls had fallen asleep, each wearing her new bracelet. The scents of shampoo and perfume still filled the air as Rebecca sat in the chair and looked at each girl. Until a few days ago, she had not known these young women, but now part of her heart belonged to them. She had given them a wonderful evening, and she knew they would wear their bracelets with pride and delight. All she could do now was pray that a time would come for each when their lives would offer them more than just the barest necessities.

A Garden of Hope

A Story from the United States

DIRECTIONS: For more information, contact: Heifer International, 1015 Louisiana Street, Little Rock, Arkansas, 72202. Visit their Web site at www.heifer.org. At the Web site you can click on "Learn," then on "Educational Resources" for activity ideas. The "Learning Centers" give children a brief tour of places in which Heifer programs are making a difference. *World Ark Online* is Heifer's news magazine that shares information about children around the world and how Heifer is helping them. Throughout the Web site are practical ways in which learners of various ages can get involved.

INTRODUCTION: In various cities, children in housing projects live in poverty and the threat of danger. With the help of adult volunteers and organizations like Heifer International, some of these children are learning work skills, confidence, direction in life, and pride. They are improving their family incomes and diets as well as beginning a path out of poverty. Since 1944, Heifer International has given training and gifts of animals that provide food and income to help people become self-reliant.

Samuel yawned and stretched. The apartment was already stifling hot. "Good morning, sleepyhead," his mother teased. She was dressed in her work uniform and was buttering toast for his two younger siblings. Little Sanura was chasing a skittering bug across the floor.

"Sanura, don't touch that ugly bug!" his mother said. She turned to Samuel. "You take good care of the little ones. No playing in the hallways. There's some cereal for dinner. Sanura and Marcus, come give me a kiss!"

She kissed the little ones, then gave further instructions, "Mind Samuel now. He's in charge when I am at work. Lock the door behind me. Don't let anyone in—not anyone. Use all the locks on the door as soon as I am gone."

Samuel sighed. She said this every morning. He knew it was because she was worried about leaving them so he tried to be patient. "Mom, I always take good care of them. But did you forget that today I start working in the garden?" Samuel said. "David said to bring the kids, too."

His mother had agreed that Samuel could join a project offered by Heifer International. A man named David taught kids business skills and responsibility through gardening and selling the produce. Samuel would make some money and bring home unsold produce, too.

His mother smiled at Samuel. "I'd forgotten. Okay, but don't take your eyes off the little ones." She blew some kisses and left.

Samuel quickly put shoes on his sister and brother and took them into the hallway. No one was hanging around, but Samuel kept watching anyway. Drug dealing was always going on somewhere nearby.

After crossing several streets, the children came to a school. In front of it was a large garden with rows of lettuce in many shades of green. Other children were there already. Some were weeding and others were harvesting the lettuce. A tall man was carefully packing the lettuce into boxes. It was David. He smiled when he saw Samuel.

"Welcome, Samuel! And who are these handsome people?" he called out.

Sanura and Marcus looked way up into David's smiling face. He shook hands with them and gave them each an apple, telling them they could play on the nearby swings. Then he showed Samuel how to harvest and pack the lettuce.

"We have three kinds of greens for today's market," David explained. "We'll go to some fancy restaurants that love to buy fresh produce. Tomorrow I'll show you how to replant where we harvested. And there's always weeding and watering! You will come five days a week, right?"

Samuel nodded. "But I have to bring the kids every time."

"No problem," David said. "Most of the other gardeners bring younger children, too. They're safer here than at home. There's plenty of trouble to get into around this neighborhood, but not any in this garden—just a lot of dirt. Now, it's market time."

The gardeners and children all gathered around David. A girl, Tamara, held a clipboard.

"We have four restaurants today. Tamara, you are in charge of showing the produce, listing prices, and taking the money," David said. "Sanura, you have the honor of being the youngest gardener here today, so you will ride on my shoulders. Let's go!"

Soon the group stopped at a restaurant in a wealthy neighborhood and met the cook.

"Ah! My favorite people!" the man exclaimed. "I'm glad to see you—look at what you've brought. Beautiful! Now, let's see what I'll need."

Samuel, with Marcus resting on his hip, watched Tamara talking prices with the cook. David said quietly to Samuel, "Listen carefully. In two weeks, this job will be yours."

When they arrived back at the garden, they divided the money and the leftover greens evenly among themselves. They then went through the work list for the next day, assigning jobs to each gardener.

"Before you leave, I have an announcement to make," David said. "You have proven to be such great workers that it's time we expand our business. Tomorrow, some people from Heifer International are coming to teach us how to take care of goats. We will learn to house, feed, and milk them, and to deliver their kids, that is, the baby goats. We'll learn how to make cheese from the goat milk, and we can sell that, too. Are you ready to take on the responsibility of being city farmers?"

A cheer went up from everyone. Even Sanura clapped her hands. She called out, "Goats! Goats!"

Samuel laughed because Sanura didn't even know what a goat was. He was happy, for somehow, through this city, farming he hoped to find a way out of the poverty his mother struggled against every day.

Eleven Years of Tears

A Story from China

DIRECTIONS: This story touches on the topic of being left out or shunned by others. Many children have this experience or fear it, so Wang Li's story offers opportunities for a discussion on accepting others. Help learners understand fully the implications for Wang Li, who is a real girl. If she had not had surgery, she would have continued to be isolated from her community, would receive no education or job training, would have suffered health problems, would not marry, and so on.

INTRODUCTION: Sometimes a baby is born with a cleft lip or palate. Before the baby is born, his or her mouth does not form correctly. This makes it very difficult for the child to eat or to speak clearly.

In many countries, fixing this condition is often a series of routine surgeries. Then the baby looks just like other babies and can easily eat and learn to speak correctly. Often, the surgery only takes a short time and does not cost very much. But many children never have the surgery because their families are too poor to pay and they live in places where no one is trained to do the surgery. As they grow up, they cannot speak in a way that others understand, they may not be sent to school, and as adults, cannot get jobs. In some places they are shunned by neighbors who believe the person's cleft problem means bad luck.

However, an organization of doctors helps these children receive the surgery they need. It is called The Smile Train (**www.smiletrain.org**). These doctors help other doctors in many parts of the world receive training to do the surgery. Then the newly-trained doctors offer medical aid to thousands of children. The organization also raises money to cover the cost of the surgery for children whose families cannot pay.

Wang Li stood just inside the doorway of her home, watching the other children on their way to school. She longed to go with them. They were chatting and laughing until one saw her. Immediately Wang Li regretted having allowed herself to be seen.

Quickly, Wang Li stepped farther back into her house but it was too late. Some of the children laughed. Others shivered. She heard them talking as they hurried on and knew they were probably talking about her.

None of them really knew her, and they never would because they wouldn't look past her face. They would never know the real Wang Li.

She could be a good student, but she was not allowed to go to school for one reason. Wang Li had been born with a cleft lip and palate.

As the voices faded, she sat down and cried. Again. There had been many years of tears in that home since Wang Li was born.

But something happened later in the day that changed Wang Li's life forever.

A stranger traveled through her village. Someone must have told him about the girl everyone shunned. The stranger found Wang Li's father. "Your daughter can be helped with a simple surgery," he said. "The organization called The Smile Train could help her."

Wang Li's father hurried home, hopeful for the first time since his daughter had been born. They began preparing for the journey to the hospital.

Together the family traveled by train, then bumped along on a bus, and after that rode on a boat. They walked the rest of the way. Finally, they reached the hospital. In a few days, Wang Li had the surgery to correct her cleft lip and palate.

The moment came when Wang Li first looked into the mirror. She cried. This time, however, she cried with happiness.

Everyone said she was beautiful. Wang Li had always been beautiful, but now it showed on the outside, too. "You look very happy!" said a nurse.

"Do you know what makes me the most happy?" Wang Li asked. "Now I can go to school! I want to be the first person in my family to go to college!"

"What would you like to study in college?"

"I want to be a doctor," she announced, and flashed a beautiful smile.

An Answer to a Prayer

A Story from South Africa

DIRECTIONS: Have the learners form small groups. Ask them to discuss the following questions.

- The man in the story says of his grandchildren, "I am all they have on this earth." Many children and teens in the world are in this situation. Given how you live and what your life is like, how do you think you would react emotionally, financially, or educationally if you were suddenly as alone as these young people?

- Oftentimes, communities that are already very poor cannot cope when a crisis occurs, such as the deaths of many adults in the community because of war or sickness. How is this different in countries where there are more resources? Name several differences.

- What do you think will happen to young people living alone, living with overburdened grandparents, or raising younger siblings themselves? What are some possibilities for their futures?

INTRODUCTION: Around the world, many children are orphaned because of the sickness AIDS. Often, grandparents are left to raise numerous children. This story speaks of one such man.

An elderly man was praying in a small church. "Dear Jesus," he said, "you know I am taking care of five of my grandchildren. I am old, so it is hard for me. I don't always have enough food for all of us. My house is only big enough for three or four people, and besides, it's ready to fall down. The older children should go to school, but it is too far to walk when their bellies are empty. But they are my grandchildren whose parents have died. I am all they have on this earth."

The man took a deep breath before going on with his prayer. "Now, Jesus, three more children need me! They are not my grandchildren but are neighbors. They, too, are alone because of this terrible sickness called AIDS, which took their parents. They are hungry and have no place to sleep. There is no one to care for them. You and I both know there are even more children like them."

Again the man paused and continued. "I know you want me to take them in, but if I do, Jesus, you will have to show me how I can do this impossible thing. I know you say all things are possible with God, but I am only one person, and an old and poor one at that. So, please show me how you plan on having me do this!"

The man stood up slowly and stepped out into the sunshine. He heard someone shout his name. Turning, he saw a young priest running toward him.

"I have good news!" the priest said. "Someone has donated some money to our church. We know you are raising your grandchildren by yourself, in a house that needs repair. If you accept, my plan is to use the money to build a house right here—for you! You and your family can move in, and the children will be closer to school. There is enough space for a large garden and even room to keep a few animals. Other people who go to our church will be close enough to help you. What do you think?"

The old man looked up toward heaven and winked.

"I think," he said, "that the Lord answers our prayers."

The Train Platform School

A Story from India

DIRECTIONS: Help students conceptualize a busy, urban train station if they have not experienced one. Then have them imagine what it would be like to sell candy there. Together, list challenges teachers would face in this type of "classroom."

INTRODUCTION: Many children in India, no longer able to live with their families, are forced to live on the streets. Some find shelter in train stations and also find work there. Some sweep floors, shine shoes, or sell newspapers, candy, or water. Others ride the trains as cleaners or baggage handlers. Because they live like this, these children don't realize that they are missing something important most other children have: an education. However, some years ago an educator recognized their need. Inderjit Khurana began the Train Platform Schools. She brought school to the children and designed the classes to fit the busy work schedules of these child laborers. Because of this, many children were able to begin regular school. Their futures were truly changed for the better. If you want to learn more about these schools, go to **www.globalfundforchildren.org**.

Every morning Rajini awoke in the train station, relieved that she had gotten through another night safely. She was always a little afraid, but more so at night. Waking early, she ran off to the place where she met the Boss Man. She had given that name to the person who paid her to sell candy at the station each day. He brought her candy each morning. Every evening he came back and collected the money she made. He paid her a small bit of money but was cross if she did not make much money that day—and he never thought she made enough.

Rajini set off with her tray of candy, knowing where to stand in the station to attract the most people. She arranged the candy nicely on the tray, then waited for the first rush of passengers. To keep from being bored, she often made up names for the people she saw regularly. There was the Man with the Big Nose, the Woman Who Wore the Prettiest Dresses, the Man Who Always Bought Chocolate, and the Young Man Who Frowned.

Every day was the same. Some people turned down her offers of candy. Most pushed past her, as though she did not exist at all. A few bought candy from her each day, and she looked for them. Her favorite was the Smiling Lady. This lady not only always bought candy, but she also spoke politely to Rajini. Rajini was amazed at that.

One day, the lady bought candy as usual. "Good morning, my Little Candy Seller!"

Rajini smiled. The lady was playing the name game, too!

"Do you ever go to school?" the Smiling Lady asked.

Rajini shook her head. She had never thought that she could go to school.

"Would you like to?"

Rajini answered shyly, "I don't know. I've never been."

"Follow me," said the woman. "I have something to show you. I have a few minutes before my train leaves."

Rajini did not know what to do. The Smiling Lady had never asked her these questions before. Was this some kind of trick or trap? She trusted no one. "In the train station?" she asked.

"Yes. Follow me," the Smiling Lady said and began weaving her way through the crowds. Rajini followed, stopping to make two sales along the way.

"Look over there," the Smiling Lady said, pointing to a group of children and one adult sitting on the train station floor. "I've asked about this. It's a school. You can go to school right here! I must leave now but please, my little friend, go over there and start school!"

Rajini stood watching as swarms of people moved around her. A school? Here, at the train station? She moved a little closer, listening to the teacher speaking about numbers.

But she must work if she was going to eat, and right now was the prime selling time. She returned to her best selling place. After a few sales, the crowd thinned out, for a train had just left the station. Another hour or so would pass before any people would be around to buy candy.

She looked back. Other child workers were hurrying over to the teacher. That is when she noticed that a large square had been drawn on the station floor with chalk. The teacher looked up and saw her watching. He smiled at her. Rajini walked a few steps closer. She looked at the children with him and recognized many of them. This gave her the courage to go over to them. The teacher motioned for her to come into the chalk square.

Rajini put her tray of candy down outside of the square, stepped over the chalk line, and began school.

Scattered Bits of Light

A Story from Germany

DIRECTIONS: This story tells of a religious tradition in parts of Europe. While the celebration is quite secular, it offers the main character a chance to reflect on spiritual matters. Help learners think about traditions and why they can hold significance for us year after year.

INTRODUCTION: Martin of Tours, France, lived around 300 AD. A well-loved European saint, his feast day, November 11, is celebrated in many towns in southern and western Germany. Called "St. Martinstag," this is mainly a children's festival, with aspects like Halloween.

The sun was low in the sky as Stefan walked home. He was laden with schoolbooks, and the load on his back matched the weight of his mood. In biology class the teacher had talked about the dwindling water supply in some countries. In social studies they had discussed the many areas around the world that were at war. Walking down the street, he had seen some graffiti that reeked of hatred. To Stefan, the world seemed darker than the shadows already cast by the setting sun.

He opened the door to the warmth of home.

Lise and Anton came running. "It's St. Martinstag!" they both shouted. Lise added, "We've started making our lanterns. And Oma's sick!"

He found his mother in the kitchen pulling on her coat. "I just got a call from your grandmother. She's not feeling well, so I must hurry over to her house."

"What about Dad?" Stefan asked.

"He's working the evening shift at the hospital, so I need you to take the little ones out for St. Martinstag. They'd be so disappointed if they couldn't go," his mother said. She smiled at Stefan apologetically. "Thanks so much, dear."

Stefan sighed. Being the eldest had its disadvantages.

He sliced a chunk of bread and poured a glass of milk, then joined the lantern makers at the table.

"When it's dark, we'll go outside with our lanterns and join everybody else. We'll sing the St. Martin songs, and then we'll go from house to house and beg for treats!" Lise said.

Anton nodded.

"We get to because of the beggar," Lise added.

"What beggar?" asked Anton.

"The beggar in the story about St. Martin, of course!"

"Oh, I don't know that," Anton said, a frown puckering his forehead.

Lise exclaimed, "If you don't know the story, you don't know why we're doing all this! Stefan, tell him! He has to know!"

Stefan sighed again, but he began, "Long ago, in the days when Roman soldiers were in Germany and France and other places, there was a soldier named Martin. When he was a little boy, he had learned about Jesus and wanted to become a Christian. But he hadn't been baptized yet.

One day when he was riding his horse, he saw a beggar, a man so poor he had to ask people for what he needed. The day was cold, and the beggar was shivering badly. He didn't have any warm clothes. Martin had on a heavy, warm cloak. So he took it off, took out his sword, and cut the cloak into two pieces. He gave half to the beggar. That night Martin had a dream. He saw the beggar wearing half the cloak. But when the beggar in the dream turned around, Martin saw that it was Jesus! Martin woke up and decided to quit being a soldier and to ask to be baptized. After that, he taught so many people about Jesus that we still remember him hundreds of years after he lived."

Anton held up his lantern. "Did St. Martin have a lantern?"

"I don't know," Lise said, frowning in thought. "But Mother says they show that Martin brought the light of Jesus to a dark world."

Anton pointed toward the window. "It's pretty dark out there now!"

Stefan smiled. Then he bundled his sister and brother into warm coats, and they soon joined the procession of children and parents. The lighted lanterns bobbed along in the children's hands, casting bits of light on the ground. As they walked, they sang songs about St. Martin. Their voices rang out in the icy night air. After the procession ended, Stefan followed Lise and Anton to their uncle's house. There they begged for treats, which they received after reciting a poem for him.

Stefan waited as they ran from house to house. He looked up into the night sky and thought of all the suffering and hatred in the world. It must have been the same when St. Martin lived. Yet Martin had not given up. He had brought a light into that dark world by being the person, the Christian, God meant him to be.

On the way home, Stefan had to carry the sleepy Anton. Lise skipped ahead, swinging both lanterns. Bits of light broke up the darkness.

Anton put his head on Stefan's shoulder. Softly, Stefan sang one more St. Martin song into the cold night air.

The Way It Used to Be

A Story from Uganda

DIRECTIONS: Two topics may be discussed with this story: family mealtimes and attitudes about food, or life in a refugee camp. With the first topic, discuss the way Mukasa's family gathered to eat, showed appreciation to the cook, and so on, perhaps comparing this to the way your learners' families share meals. Help them see the beauty in the Ugandan customs. Discuss reverence for food in general and the need for this.

If you choose to focus on the refugee camp, have learners imagine themselves in Mukasa's place. What do they think they would do to occupy themselves? Have they ever experienced fear and drastic life changes as Mukasa has? What would they miss if they were suddenly relocated and had to leave almost everything behind?

INTRODUCTION: Uganda is a country rich in resources, but several decades of fighting have ravaged the country. Many peaceful Ugandans have had their lives disrupted and changed forever. We need to recognize the happy aspects of life in Uganda during peaceful times, as well as be aware of the suffering of the people during the periods of war and civil unrest.

Mukasa lay on his mat, his arm covering his face to keep the sun out. It wasn't time to sleep, but there was nothing else to do. At home he would have taken care of the goats and spent time with friends. At night, there were always stories by the fire.

He remembered it all. In their village, everyone worked hard, but they produced plenty of food. If he tried, he could almost smell the cooking aromas from his mother's open fire stove. She and his sisters cooked bananas, sweet potatoes, cabbage, or tomatoes. They also cooked with white potatoes, beans, peas, peanuts, onions, and pumpkins. If he was hungry between meals, he had plenty of fruit, like oranges and papayas, to snack on.

His whole family would sit down on straw mats to eat. First they washed their hands. Then they enjoyed their meal. Mukasa remembered how, when he was younger, he wanted to run and play just as soon as he had eaten. But he had to learn, as all children did, that one always stayed seated until everyone finished eating. That showed respect for the food. Then, one by one, they would thank his mother for preparing it. Many evenings they sat around a fire, and the grandmothers and grandfathers would tell stories. Mukasa learned history from those stories. He was taught what was important to his people, how best to act, and what was expected of him.

But now, everything was different.

A corrupt leader in their country had led different groups of people to fighting among themselves. Mukasa's family was no longer safe in their home. They had to leave everything behind to flee from the violence. They had then come to this refugee camp.

So had thousands of other families. All hours of the day and night, as far as you could see, there were people. When it was time to sleep, his family members lay side by side, with only plastic sheeting above to protect them from the rain.

Now they waited in long lines for water. His parents were gone for hours at a time trying to get food. There were no animals to care for, no food from the animals, no garden, no fruit trees. No work, no fun.

He missed the meals the most. Not only was he hungry more often now, but he missed sitting with his family, talking and laughing. They were scattered now. One sister had gone off with a soldier. His older brother had become a soldier. His grandfather had died. His father smiled less and less, and his mother's beautiful eyes were filled with worry and weariness.

He also missed the evening fires. He and his family were not allowed to gather, to stay up after dark and talk. No longer could the elders pass on stories.

Mukasa rolled onto his side. There was no point in getting up. He knew he was missing the life he was supposed to live.

Hanging On

A Story from India

DIRECTIONS: Part of understanding injustice is the ability to imagine another person's suffering. This story, which tells of a dangerous job carried out by a destitute child, details many of the physical sensations the main character experiences in the course of a day. Discuss these with the learners and as a group, imagining what the rest of his week might be like.

INTRODUCTION: In many parts of the world, even the United States, children are forced to work at dangerous jobs. This story describes one such job that many boys have to take so they can buy food.

Horns honked, bicycles swerved in and out between cars, and people darted and ran. Everyone was trying to use the road at once.

A boy stood on the street corner. The smells of exhaust, sweat, and food swirled around him along with the dust. He was hungry, and he had no place to sleep tonight.

A tempo pulled up beside him. It looked like a minivan with the back door taken off and was used as a taxi. The driver leaned out his window and called, "Want a job? I need some help."

The boy was so hungry, he didn't ask what the job was. He jumped into the front seat. The driver looked at him as if he were crazy.

"Don't sit here!" he bellowed at the boy. "Don't you know what to do?"

The boy shook his head.

The driver rolled his eyes. "Go get on in the back. Don't sit down. Every seat is for a paying passenger. You collect the fares as the people get off. You grab anyone who tries to leave without paying. In a few days, you'll be announcing the stops, but I'll do that today. Get back there now!"

The boy went around to the back of the tempo. He pulled himself up by grabbing the doorframe where the door had once been. In a moment, people started getting on through the back. The boy tried to make himself small as they crowded on. The driver, he knew, was watching him in the rearview mirror.

When the tempo started up, the boy fell backward. Desperately, he grabbed the doorframe. This, he realized, was the only way he was going to keep himself on the tempo. If he fell out on these crowded roads, he would surely be run over by whatever vehicle was right behind the tempo.

For the rest of the day, he clung to the doorframe as the driver wove in and out of the traffic, swerving to avoid bicycles, slamming on his brakes to stop for passengers. As the first passengers of the day were getting off, the driver yelled, "Hey back there! Get the fares!"

The boy uncurled his fingers from the doorframe and put out his hands. Everyone dropped coins into them and jumped off. Others got on and the tempo took off again, the boy trying to keep the money with him and still hold on.

Around the city and its people, the tempo raced, braked, stopped, and swerved for hours. Though still hungry, the boy began feeling sick to his stomach as he inhaled the gas fumes.

At one stop, a young man pushed past others who were paying their fares. He jumped off the tempo and started to run.

"Hey!" the driver bellowed. "Catch him! He never paid!"

Confused and nauseated, the boy didn't know what to do with the fares he had collected.

"He's getting away!" the driver boomed. "Go!"

The young man was soon lost in the crowd by now, but the boy dropped the money onto a seat to run after him. He didn't know what he would do if he did catch the man. The boy soon stopped however, because it occurred to him the tempo driver might leave without paying him for this day's work. He ran back to the tempo where the driver was standing outside, glaring at him.

"Lost him," the boy said, his head pounding, his stomach lurching.

"Of course you lost him—you stood there like a great lunk! Forget tomorrow. I don't want you back," the driver snarled and got back into the tempo.

The boy stuck his head in the window. He was frightened but hunger made him speak up. "I want my payment for today."

"Don't deserve any," the driver muttered, but dropped a few coins into the boy's outstretched hand and started up the tempo.

As the driver sped off, the boy looked around. He realized he didn't know where he was in the city now.

"Hey," said a voice behind him.

He whirled around. There stood another boy who asked, "First day on a tempo?"

The boy nodded. "Maybe the last."

"There are plenty of other tempos," the other boy said. "I knew the kid who used to work that one."

"Did he find a better driver to work for?" the boy asked hopefully.

His companion laughed. "There are no better drivers. No, the kid I knew, he fell out the back and was run over. Broke his leg and some ribs."

"Oh."

"Come on," said his new friend. "I know a place where we can get some sleep. And tomorrow's another day."

The Runaway

A Story from the United States

DIRECTIONS: After reading the story, visit www.covenanthouseny.org to read more about the good work done by Covenant House and how your learners can help, including hosting a virtual vigil.

INTRODUCTION: This fictional story is based on real circumstances. Since the beginning of Covenant House in New York in 1972, the organization has helped more that 500,000 children and has expanded to fourteen more cities in the United States as well as Canada and Latin America. Covenant House provides homeless and runaway youth with food, shelter, clothing, and crisis care, as well as health care, education, vocational preparation, legal help, drug abuse treatment and prevention programs, and many other services.

It was snowing lightly. A few Christmas lights twinkled from a storefront. Thirteen-year-old Tyrone saw the van coming down the street. Other kids had told him about this van. It came from Covenant House, a place that helped kids who were in trouble, kids who lived on the streets, kids who were runaways.

Well, he fit the description. When his mother died, Tyrone had gone to live with his aunt. One of her friends was a man who often came to visit. But he was no friend to Tyrone. In fact, sometimes he hurt Tyrone. Tyrone never knew what to expect. He told his aunt, but she said, "If you don't like it here, you don't have to stay."

So Tyrone left, with very little money, no luggage, no place to go, and no plan. After a few nights of sleeping in a bus station, he found some kids who lived in an abandoned building. Glass lay on the floor beneath broken windows, and it was always cold. Cockroaches and rats scurried about. Some of the older kids tried to hurt the younger kids. Usually everybody was at least a little hungry.

One boy said that the Covenant House van always had food for kids like them. Another said

you could trust the people who drove the van. Tyrone didn't know whom he could trust.

Snow was falling down the back of his neck now. Tyrone pulled the collar of his jacket up as the van came closer. His stomach rumbled, but the fear in his stomach grew stronger than the hunger. He wouldn't get inside the van. If they were willing to give him food outside the van, great. Otherwise, he would forget it.

The van stopped and a woman got out. "Hi," she said. "My name is Keshia. I'm from Covenant House. I've got some sandwiches in the van. Want some?"

Tyrone looked at her. He backed up a few steps. "I'm kind of hungry," he said quietly. He shivered a little.

"I've got some hot chocolate, too," she offered. "You could get warm in the van."

"No," Tyrone said, turning to leave.

"I'll bring them out here then," she called after him. He stopped.

Soon he had eaten three sandwiches and he drank two cups of steaming hot chocolate while standing several feet from the van.

"Maybe I'll see you another time," Keshia said. "I usually drive around here and I always have food."

Tyrone didn't say anything. He stepped back into the shadow of a building as the van left. He was still cold and he wasn't sure if he would go back to sleep in the old building, but at least he wasn't hungry.

Tyrone let a week pass before he looked for the van again. After that, he became sort of a regular, getting a meal a few times a week from the people who drove the Covenant House van. Besides Keshia, there were Jack and Miguel. They talked with him, shared some laughs, and gave him a card with the Covenant House number on it. He told them his first name. Still, he would not enter the van. He couldn't be sure there wasn't some trick to all this. As Christmas drew closer, the weather grew colder. Tyrone walked down the street, hunched over in the wind. His head hurt, and so did his throat. He thought he might have a fever. Maybe tonight he would sleep in the bus station. He sat down on a bus stop bench and tucked his legs under him to warm his feet a little. A nearby store was blaring Christmas carols, and the song, "I'll Be Home for Christmas" came on. Tyrone wiped his nose on his sleeve and waited for the Covenant House sandwiches.

A man came up to the bench. "Hey, kid, want to make some quick money?" he asked.

Tyrone looked up. All of his nerves felt electric. This man meant trouble, big trouble.

Just then, the van rounded the corner. "My ride's here," Tyrone said.

He jumped up and waved to the van. It pulled up, and the man fled into the darkness. Tyrone did not wait for Keshia to get out but jumped into the van.

"Tyrone, did that man hurt you?" Keshia asked quickly.

Tyrone shook his head. "Didn't have a chance," he said. He was shivering all over, and it was not just from cold.

"You had a narrow escape, my friend," Jack said. "Why don't you ride around with us for awhile until we're sure that guy is gone?"

Tyrone could only nod because his mouth was full of food. Miguel pulled away from the curb. Tyrone sipped the chocolate, his throat burning and his head pounding. Slowly his feet began to tingle and ache as the heat in the van warmed him. Still, he felt more comfortable than he had in months.

And he felt safe. After finishing his food, he put his head back a little and half-closed his eyes.

"A kid never deserves to be hurt, or homeless, or hungry," Miguel said as he drove.

Tyrone remained silent, but he was listening.

"At Covenant House, lots of kids can get help, depending on their age and situation," Jack said.

After a few minutes of silence, Tyrone said, "Take me there. Please."

"We're on our way," Miguel said and turned a corner. He flipped on the radio.

"O holy night…" a Christmas carol came over the radio.

But Tyrone never heard it. He was fast asleep.

For Lack of Water and Justice

A Story from Sudan

DIRECTIONS: Divide the class into two groups. Assist one group to discuss (or write) about the justice issues in this story. Encourage them to look at the issues in light of the principles of Catholic social teaching. In the meantime, have the other group discuss Amani's emotional and physical experiences and speculate on the future of her family. Come together to share the insights both groups now have.

INTRODUCTION: This story takes place in western Sudan where a very complicated situation has resulted in fighting among groups within the country. Civilians are often targeted, and, in addition to violence, hunger plays a huge part in the vast numbers of deaths.

More than one million people have left their homes because of the attacks and the lack of food. Refugee camps are crowded and resources scarce.

In addition to war, the Sudanese people have suffered greatly because of a severe drought. Water holes have dried up, the bodies of dead animals have poisoned many wells, and the government, involved in war, has neglected the nation's water system, so many wells no longer function.

The sun had not yet risen when Amani set out for the only hand-pump in the area. She was to bring back her family's supply of water for the day. While she dreaded the unrelenting sunshine beating down on her head and shoulders, the darkness held its own miseries. She never knew when a soldier might be lurking in this darkness. Carrying the empty water jug, she hurried along, alert to any movement or noise that might bring danger.

She had hoped her younger sister, Asmina, could come with her, but Asmina was sick. With water scarce, the family could not drink sufficient water or wash regularly, so each of them was in danger of illness. Weakened already by too little food and water, Asmina had become sick very quickly. Amani knew that young children did not survive long under these conditions, and she hoped fervently the water she brought could help.

As the first light of dawn touched the sky, she could tell where the pump was by the crowd of people around it. Hundreds of people, maybe more, were waiting. Once again, it would take her all day to get water.

Amani approached the crowd. She heard many voices, murmuring, gossiping, arguing, and crying—the sounds of people waiting, waiting, waiting. She joined the long line and watched the sun's progress. Soon the heat of the day was adding to her thirst. Amani thought of her little sister, suffering more than she was. She thought of school, which she could no longer attend. She loved school and had stopped going only when food was so scarce that she was too hungry to concentrate. Since the thousands of refugees had arrived and the water had begun to run low, she had not gone to school at all. She spent each day, the entire day, getting water.

A few hours later, Amani had made some progress in line. Maybe in the next hour she would get to the pump. Then, before she could react, a man came up to her and pushed her. She fell onto her water jug. Looking up she could see the hard expression on his face. Fear, thirst, and other suffering had left this man desperate. Amani could not possibly fight for her place in line.

Wearily, she made her way back to the end of the line. Anger, frustration, hunger, and thirst welled up inside of her. She wanted to scream, she wanted to cry. But she needed all her energy to carry the water, when she got it, back home.

Time for School

A Story from Pakistan

DIRECTIONS: Encourage learners to look up countries where girls' school attendance is lower than other places of that region. See what steps are being taken to remedy this problem. One source of information can be found at the Web site for World Bank, **www.worldbank.org**.

INTRODUCTION: In the country of Pakistan, less than half of the adult population can read. Some sources say it may only be twenty-six percent, and the number is even lower for girls and women. In rural areas, obtaining an education is especially difficult for girls. Traditionally, girls are not sent to school. Also, a greatly mistaken belief is that the religion of Islam does not allow girls to be educated. With the help of groups who understand that Islam supports girls' education, that situation is slowly changing. Families are always better off if the mother has attended school. Following is a story of one lucky Pakistani girl who will go to school.

Jamila remembered the night a year ago, when she awoke because she had heard her parents' voices.

"I've decided we have been wrong not to send our daughters to school," her father had said.

Instantly, Jamila was fully awake.

"Each meeting I go to, I understand better how it will help a whole family to have the mother educated."

"Do you want Jamila to learn to read?" Jamila could hear the surprise in her mother's question.

"Yes," her father said in his most stubborn voice. "Maybe she can then teach Palwasha and Khanzadi."

Now her mother sounded alarmed. "But they are both betrothed, and neither of their husbands' families want wives who can read!"

"I intend to talk with them about this. At the meeting, the leader read from our holy book. It clearly says that both men and women should be educated. In fact, we made plans tonight to start building a school. Both boys and girls will be educated in our town!" Jamila's father said. "To hear that man reading the sacred words, words I cannot read myself—well, I knew then that we must not keep our children from this knowledge."

"You don't think it is a waste of time to read when they can raise their families by fishing or farming?"

"No. Tonight I learned that knowledge is never a waste of time. I wish I could read. I wish you could, too," her father said. "But let's start with Jamila."

Jamila grinned with joy. Her one wish for her life would be fulfilled!

That was a year ago. In the days following that conversation, her father had gone from house to house in their town, convincing parents and grandparents that they should enroll their children in a school that would be built, with a section for girls and a section for boys.

Next he convinced them to work together to build the school. Furniture was made, too. A group formed to hire a teacher. Another worked to get school supplies for the children. Plans were made for adult classes to be held at the school in the evenings.

After all that work and planning, the first day of school came. Jamila walked down the path, away from her home. Her eyes shown with excitement as she turned to look back at her parents standing in the doorway. Her mother was smiling broadly, her father was solemn and proud.

She waved and then turned back to the path to the school, the path to her new future.

The Performance

A Story from the Ukraine

DIRECTIONS: Have learners name different ways in which they are creative. Encourage a wide definition of creativity. Suggest some ideas to start the discussion, such as finding clever ways to distract a crying child while babysitting, planning a birthday party with a mystery theme, giving Christmas gifts without spending more than $5. Then talk about how it feels to be so creative.

Discuss how creativity has been used in history to improve life. Think in terms of medical advancements, cultural accomplishments, and political strategy.

For more information about young people such as those in this story, go to **www.havenbridge.org**.

INTRODUCTION: This story takes place in Eastern Europe, where the end of Communist rule has left countless people greatly impoverished. Because of this, many children live in orphanages, and the orphanages do not always have many supplies. However, creative orphanage directors manage to bring in volunteer music teachers, find inexpensive ways to offer sports that require minimal equipment, and may even be able to send children as exchange students to other countries. They also encourage the children to find their own ways of being creative despite lack of materials. "The Performance" is based on life in a real orphanage, where the creativity of the teens is remarkable.

Scene One: The Plan

In a girls' bedroom in the orphanage, six single beds were lined up in three rows. The headboards were wooden, old, and chipped, but most were brightened by a myriad of small photos taped to them. These beds were made so neatly, they would have passed inspection in any army. Each had a pastel-colored bedspread, and the pillows were placed at the head of the bed to look like dollops of whipped cream. The single window was graced with a soft white curtain, but the walls were bare of any decoration. A few scatter rugs lay on the wooden floor.

Despite the sparseness, there was no lack of creativity in this room. On two of the beds sat three girls, talking quickly and excitedly.

"We have four days to put this show together," Nastya said. "If we use some of the things we have already done, we might have time to make up some new things."

"This program is for visitors from the States. They would probably like to hear our folk songs," Alyona said.

"Get out the traditional costumes we made," Anya said.

"And our folk dances, especially the kyorovody. Everybody loves that gentle and calm dance," Alyona added.

"Keep the costumes on," Anya quipped.

"We'd better ask Katya if the costumes need any repair. I think mine ripped last time," Nastya said. "But we don't want to do all traditional things. Everybody loves it when Lida sings "Wild Dances." She looks just like the famous Ruslana* and everyone goes wild singing with her!"

Just then, Lida entered the room. "Talking about me?" she asked, and then, swinging her long dark hair, went into a rendition of "Wild Dance." As she leaped and danced around the beds, singing in a clear, strong voice, the other girls joined her, arms waving, hair flying, voices blending.

When this impromptu performance was over, the girls collapsed in giggles on the bed. But Nastya was relentless in her organizing. "You will definitely sing that for the show?"

"If I can catch my breath by then!" Lida said.

Alyona sat up. "And if we are doing that, let's do the dance you made up, Anya." She paused and closed her eyes, remembering the experience. "Oh, how I loved dancing that with the others, everyone in black and you in the center in white.

It's so beautiful!" Still sitting, she waved her arms, remembering the grace of the dance.

Anya smiled. She loved to create dances as much as she loved dancing.

The bell rang for dinner, and they hurried to the dining room. The girls gathered their trays, which held bowls of a thick potato soup and a plate of cucumbers and tomatoes. At each table, one child was assigned to get the spoons and cups of milk and to set the table. This evening the assignment fell to Sergai.

Nastya watched him as he balanced a thick slice of buttered bread on top of each cup. Alyona watched Nastya watching Sergai. She knew what was coming next.

"Sergai, would you and your brother Vanya be up for a little wrestling?"

Sergai shrugged his shoulders. "We usually are."

"For a performance?" Nastya asked. "For some people from the States."

Again the shrug. "I'll ask Vanya. I don't see why not."

"We can ask Katya to do her gymnastics," Alyona said, then put down her spoon. "Wait! What day is the performance?"

"February 14," Nastya said. "That gives us plenty of time—"

Alyona persisted. "That's Valentine's Day! Part of the show could be around that!"

Nastya was looking at Sergai again, who was now eating his soup. Anya and Alyona were looking around at the other boys. Then they looked at each other. Planning had begun.

Scene Two: Going a Bit Too Far

In four days' time, they came up with songs and dances about love, marriage, and a bit about the man called St. Valentine. Anya was devoting all her spare time to teaching the new dances. She convinced Reuben to help her bring some new moves into the dances. Reuben had taught himself to dance as well as speak English by watching American movies.

Alyona and Nastya wrote a skit to mimic a television dating game show. Lida was to be the host, asking questions of three "couples." They laughed and groaned and giggled as they came up with silly and funny questions and answers. Nastya had to do some fast-talking to get Sergai, Reuben, and their friend Andre to play the male characters.

"Now for costumes," Alyona said to Katya one evening as they sat in the common room. "Something romantic, something..." She paused, grasping for ideas.

"Something bridal," Katya said. "Something white with lace."

"We have white dresses," Alyona said. "But lace?"

Katya looked at the windows with a mischievous smile. "Those curtains would do nicely."

"Ooooh," said Alyona breathlessly. "Nice touch but big trouble. We can't just take curtains down and make them into costumes without someone getting really angry with us!"

"I know there is no lace in our fabric box," Katya said simply. "We could use the curtains and not sew them or cut them. I'll figure out a way to add them to the dresses without hurting the curtains. Or we might use them for veils." She had her hands on the curtains already.

Alyona sighed. Between Katya's flair for creative costumes and Nastya's drive for a great performance, she knew she was going to get into trouble. But oh, how romantic Katya could make the dresses look if only they had some lace! She went over and helped Katya take down the curtains.

Anya was delighted. She tossed a curtain into the air. "These will flow so nicely in the dances! Great idea, Katya!"

"Yes, but…" Alyona tried to protest.

"Nobody will even notice they're gone," Nastya said. "I never noticed them—where did you get them?"

"Oh, come on, Nastya! Do you really think nobody will notice?" Alyona asked nervously.

Nastya shrugged. "I have no idea where you got them from. Why should anyone else?"

"Think how graceful you will look," Anya said, laying a curtain across Alyona's shoulders.

The lacy curtain felt like a silken spider's web settling on her shoulders. Alyona gave one last, worried look at the door, and took part in planning.

A day later, all the girls were seated in Sveta's classroom. The teacher was pacing back and forth in front of them. Even her shoes seemed angry.

"Curtains do not just come off the rods by themselves and disappear," she said. "I know you have a show coming up and I know you make marvelous costumes. Therefore I am asking you where the curtains are. I want an honest answer right now."

The girls shifted uneasily until Katya said, "They are part of the costumes—but really, they will be fine to use after the performance! They aren't cut or anything! We'll put them right back up afterward—I promise!"

Sveta kept walking back and forth, as if she were marching. "Whose idea was this?"

Again Katya spoke, "Mine."

The other girls looked at each other.

"But it was my idea to have costumes that looked like brides' dresses, and you really need lace for that," Alyona said meekly.

"And I encouraged them because I wanted costumes that would flow when they danced," Anya admitted.

"And, well, I'm involved, too," Nastya said.

"You have broken several rules and may ruin the curtains. For this you will not be allowed to leave the building for four days. And you will wash the curtains, make any needed repair to them, and rehang them after the performance," Sveta said firmly.

Alyona looked up and asked, "Does this mean we can use the curtains?"

"I never said so in those words. Now go—you have a lot of work to do before this performance," Sveta said.

As the girls left the room, Nastya said, "I still can't believe anyone noticed they were gone!"

Scene Three: A Class Act

The folk dances were charming, the acrobatics and wrestling impressive. Now the audience was laughing over Lida's ridiculous questions to the three "couples" dressed in bridal clothes. Alyona could feel the lace curtain on her head and shoulders and she knew she looked beautiful. Reuben, holding her arm, had just delivered a funny line when Alyona caught sight of Sveta in the audience.

Sveta's arms were crossed, but she was smiling. And when she caught Alyona looking at her, she gave her a thumbs-up sign.

---

* Ruslana's unique performance and song, "Wild Dance," won the 2004 Eurovision Song Contest. She was the first Ukrainian to win. She has also served as a Good Will Ambassador for UNICEF.

The Gift

A Story from Bangladesh and the United States

DIRECTIONS: Designate two readers for this story.

Reader 1 This is the story of two girls. Megan lives in the United States, and Dalki lives in Bangladesh. They have two things in common: both are ten years old and both have held a certain yellow sweatshirt in their hands.

Reader 2 Megan woke up on the morning of her birthday. She was ten years old now! She bounded out of bed and hurried to the kitchen where her father was making a big breakfast.

"Happy birthday!" he greeted her. "Blueberry pancakes for the birthday girl!"

Reader 1 In Bangladesh, Dalki was up early. She had to get to her sewing machine in the factory early enough to get in fifteen hours of work that day. In the noisy factory, she took her place along with many other girls. Dalki picked up the yellow sweatshirt fabric and began to sew.

Reader 2 A pile of brightly wrapped gifts lay at Megan's place. She could hardly finish her pancakes because she wanted to open her presents.

Reader 1 Dalki's stomach rumbled. Her head felt a little dizzy because she had not eaten since the night before. Still, she kept sewing, for she feared the man who ran the factory.

Reader 2 First Megan opened an envelope from her uncle. "Twenty-five dollars!" she exclaimed. "Now I can buy that shirt I've been wanting!"

Her parents smiled. "Go on, open the present from Grandma," her mother urged.

Reader 1 Dalki worked as quickly as she could. For each finished shirt, she was paid five cents. She didn't know that the shirts she made were sold in stores for more than seventeen dollars.

What she did know was that she never had a day off. After fifteen hours of work every day, she had no time for fun or school.

Reader 2 Megan tore open the tissue paper. There, neatly folded, was a yellow sweatshirt. On the front was a grinning face of a cartoon character Megan liked.

"Awesome!" Megan shouted and pulled the shirt on over her head.

Reader 1 Dalki had now been at the sewing machine for several hours and her shoulders ached. She felt the pain of hunger in her stomach. She blinked her eyes to see better. Then her fingers slipped and the machine cut a tiny hole in the fabric.

The boss was right there. With the back of his hand, he slapped Dalki across her head. She slumped forward, and he grabbed her by the back of her shirt. "You do that again and you'll get worse, do you hear?"

Dalki nodded, her head pounding, her hands shaking.

Reader 2 Megan rubbed her hands on the arms of the cozy cloth. "I love it! I'll go call Grandma to thank her!"

"Tell her we'll meet her for lunch after you and I go shopping," her mother called after Megan.

Reader 1 Dalki went on sewing the yellow fabric, adding the piece that had a face of a cartoon character on it. She still had ten more hours to work.

An Open Field

A Story from Cambodia

DIRECTIONS: Ask the learners to explore the topic of land mines left in the ground and the effects they have on people's lives. Suggest sites such as the World Health Organization (www.who.int/en/), CARE (www.care.org), and UNICEF (www.unicef.org). On these sites, go to "search" and type "land mines."

Suggest that learners use the information they have acquired to make others aware of this problem, or to raise money to contribute to safety education programs, or when meeting with elected officials to urge support of the mine ban treaty, and so on.

INTRODUCTION: In Cambodia, Vietnam, and many other countries, people are endangered by "leftovers" of wars. These leftovers are explosives that have not been set off (bombs, mines, cluster munitions, grenades, shells, rockets, and so on). One estimate says eighty million such explosives still exist. These devices can remain active for more than fifty years.

The different kinds and sizes of explosives share these common factors: they are all buried and have the potential to cause tremendous harm, including death or serious injury to people.

An atmosphere of fear develops. Many explosives were planted near water sources and along roads, preventing people from planting crops, going to wells, getting to doctors, and so on. The result is hunger and disease. With restricted access to roads, water sources, social services, and food, people are prevented from making a livable wage.

"An Open Field" and "The Hero" address problems in different countries, but each circumstance is due to these explosives.

Meas was walking home from school when she noticed people in the field by her home. They were wearing protective clothing and carrying equipment Meas did not recognize. They seemed to be searching for something and they were moving carefully.

She wondered how they could go into that field. Every single day, Meas' parents and grandparents warned her that she must never, under any circumstances, go into that field. There was

danger in that field. She could be badly hurt or even killed if she went into it.

Meas wanted to know more, but children were not allowed to speak until an adult spoke to them. She already knew that the search had something to do with explosives. Most of her classmates told stories of uncles, grandmothers, or neighbors who had been badly injured in explosions. But no one in her family seemed willing to say anything other than, "Stay away from the field and the river bank, too!" Certain roads were forbidden to her also.

Once home, Meas climbed up the ladder to her house built on stilts. It was up high so when the big rains came each year, the house would not be washed away.

Grandfather was home. He smiled at her, but as always she noticed the sadness in his eyes.

"Did you come straight home from school?" he asked. "Did you go near the field?"

"I came right home from school. I will never go near the field or the riverbank," she answered.

"Good," he said. He looked out toward the field. "Do you know what 'land mines' are?"

"Are they some things in the ground that explode and hurt people?"

"Yes, but they don't belong in the ground. Soldiers hid them there when our country was at war. There are millions in the ground all over our country. You know, in war people kill each other. One of the ways is by 'planting' these land mines. Some are only about this big," he said, making a large "O" shape with the fingers of both his hands. "But when a person steps on one, it blows up. And the person who steps on it is badly hurt, or even killed."

"Do you know anyone who has been hurt by one?" Meas asked, relieved to finally be talking about this.

"My older brother, Khuon," Grandfather said. "He was plowing the field when he stepped on one. He lost his left leg and was badly burned. He suffered for a long time. Even when he could walk on crutches, he was always afraid. He never went anywhere or wanted to see anyone. He had bad dreams for years."

Meas remained silent, sensing her grandfather's pain at the memories. Then he went on, "But Khuon survived. He lived to be an old man. Others never had that chance. I had another granddaughter. She was your cousin and would be a young woman now. She was such a dear little one! One day she decided to pick some flowers by the river. Young children are so small; they don't have much chance against a mine, but those of us left behind must go on. See those people out there? They are trained to go into fields and clear the land of mines. It is very dangerous work, but until the mines are cleared, we can't use the field."

Meas looked up quickly at her grandfather. "That's our field?" she asked.

"Yes. We thought if you knew it was our field, you might be more likely to go into it, so we never told you. We haven't been able to plant it for years. In times when we haven't made much money in other ways, we didn't dare use the field for crops. And then we went hungry."

Meas nodded. She knew what hunger meant.

Grandfather said, "But that's changing now. These people will rid our field of all danger, and then we can plant there. Imagine it this time next year!"

Meas looked from the field to her grandfather. He was smiling and Meas noticed that his eyes did not look quite so sad now.

The Hero

A Story from Vietnam

DIRECTIONS: After reading the story, have students find the answers to these questions:

- Why did the United States go to war in Vietnam?

- Four presidents had terms during this war: Dwight Eisenhower, John F. Kennedy, Lyndon Johnson, and Richard Nixon. What plans for Vietnam did each carry out?

- What was the response of the American people to this war?

- How did the war end?

- Who won this war?

INTRODUCTION: Vietnam is one of many countries plagued by land mines and other explosives as a result of the Vietnam War in which the United States was involved.

Here are a few facts about the Vietnam War:

- What Americans call the Vietnam War is also known as the Second Indochina War. It occurred over the years 1954 to 1975. This war grew out of a conflict between France and Vietnam. For 100 years, France ruled Vietnam. In 1954, the Vietnamese forced France out of power.

- Many international events happening at that time affected decisions made about Vietnam. Several countries, including the United States, had differing ideas about war-torn Vietnam's future. The unfortunate result divided Vietnam and caused yet another war which lasted eleven years. The United States was heavily involved.

- By some statistics, this war caused the death of three to five million people.

For Anh Dung, the school day started as usual. He and his many schoolmates exercised in long rows outside before going in for their lessons. But he was surprised when his teacher handed him a new textbook. It was all about *bom-min*, the Vietnamese word for unexploded devices, such as mines.

"We are first going to learn about bom-min and the great danger they hold for us. Then we will write, draw, and create plays about what we have learned. After that, we'll put on a program for your parents and other adults in our town. You will be the teachers that day!"

Anh Dung knew that these explosives were leftovers from a long-ago war. He knew they were dangerous and had been warned many times by adults not to touch anything on the ground that he did not recognize. Now he was taught how to recognize different kinds. An uneasy feeling began in his stomach. He knew he had seen parts of these before, and they had been in his very own house.

Before he could think further on this, his teacher began explaining how accidents happened with bom-min, and how to avoid them.

As he read further about accidents, Anh Dung remembered a man who lived not far from his house. The man usually stayed in the house, but the few times Anh Dung had seen him, he had been upset when he noticed the man had a terribly scarred face. One eye seemed permanently shut, and part of his right arm was missing, too. When Anh Dung had asked about their neighbor, his mother had shushed him. "It's wrong to pay attention to someone who is so different," she said as her only explanation. He had been a young child then and had never asked again. But now he wondered if this man had been a victim of bom-min.

At home, Anh Dung cautiously asked his father about bom-min. "Whatever kind they are, they are extremely dangerous. Don't any of you children go near one," was his father's prompt reply.

Anh Dung's younger brother and sisters nodded. They too were learning about them in school. But Anh Dung pushed a little more. "That man who lives nearby—the one with the scarred face and only part of his right arm—was he hurt by a mine or a grenade?" He hoped to find out why he had seen some at their house.

"Do not speak of him," his mother said firmly, and placed a large bowl of noodles on the table. Anh Dung felt his father's eyes on him.

At school, they proceeded with the projects. The younger children were learning songs. Some of his classmates wrote poems, stories, and essays. One group practiced skits. Anh Dung and a few others worked hard creating posters. To do this, he had to learn even more about where explosives had been laid—along roads, in fields and forests, beside wells, along riverbanks, and even in some buildings. As he drew and painted, he looked closely at his textbook and knew for certain he had seen his father working on some kind of explosive. But why? Why would he endanger himself and his family? Anh Dung felt anger well up within him. As he created paintings of people badly hurt, fear grew inside him. He had to speak to his father.

A few days later, he found his father bending over some pieces of metal. Anh Dung knew immediately what they were. Terribly frightened, he demanded, "What are you doing? We could get killed—all of us! You told me never to go near one of these things, but here you have brought one into the house!" His voice was high and tight. Had those words even come out of him?

The look on his father's face told Anh Dung that he had stepped across an important boundary. Children never, ever spoke to their parents in the way Anh Dung had just done.

His father was furious, and his mother came running. She saw the fear on Anh Dung's face, the pieces of metal on the table, and her husband's anger. "Go get the little ones ready for school," she instructed Anh Dung.

He did so, but could hear his parents talking in quiet voices. "We need the money," his father said.

Anh Dung now understood that his father was taking bombs or other explosives apart so he could sell the parts. He understood, but he was no less afraid.

The day of the program had come. Parents, grandparents, and other townspeople arrived at the school. Both of Anh Dung's parents were in the audience. His little brother stood with his class and sang songs about bom-min. One sister recited a poem she had written. His other sister acted in a skit of a game show. Everyone enjoyed this even though they were learning facts while they played. Then Anh Dung performed in a skit about the dangers of taking bon-min apart. Later, he saw his parents carefully examining the posters he had painted.

Many guests complimented the teachers and students on their work. Anh Dung's father smiled and nodded at his children and then left.

Later that evening, his mother came to Anh Dung as he studied. "Your father and I have been talking. He wants you to know that he always disconnected those explosives before he brought them home. In the house, he only took the other parts off. He never endangered the rest of us, only himself. He did it because we need more money. He is sorry that he frightened you."

"I'm still frightened for him!" Anh Dung said.

His mother nodded. "We talked all the way home about what your teachers have taught you. While your father knew what he was doing was dangerous, he was willing to take the risk to support us. Seeing and listening to our children today made him think about how much harder it would be for us if he were hurt or worse, so we decided that I am going to go back to being a street vendor with our vegetables. Maybe that will help enough so he can stop this dangerous work. Then he will be able to look for better work so we both can bring in more money."

"I'll take care of the children after school so you can be gone during the day," Anh Dung offered.

His mother smiled. "We chose your name because it means 'strong hero.' You've been a hero for our family. And you are also a very good son. Go back to your homework now," she said, but paused to hug him before she left to prepare their dinner.

Worth the Wait

A Story from El Salvador

DIRECTIONS: Brainstorm as a group as to how many ways a family uses water each day. Help students research which countries are experiencing serious water shortages. Find comparisons of daily water use by individuals in different countries. (On the Internet, use phrases like "water shortages" and "water usage by country.") Challenge students to cut down their families' water use for one week. At the end of the week, add up how much water was saved by the efforts of the families of your class.

INTRODUCTION: A shortage of drinking water is a growing world problem. El Salvador is one of the countries where lack of water is already a serious issue. "Worth the Wait" describes the life of persons who truly appreciate the gift of water.

Catarina and her younger sister walked barefoot down the dusty road. Little Evelyn walked slowly, lagging behind Catarina. Every few steps, Evelyn complained, "I'm thirsty! And I'm hungry!"

"Then the sooner we get to the comedor the better," Catarina said. She stopped and waited for Evelyn to catch up, then took her sister's hand. "It's not much further now, you know."

The comedor was a small building where food was served to the children of the town. Many of the families were very poor and often did not have enough food. At the comedor or dining room, the children came to eat a healthy meal each day. The comedor was run by Hermana (Sister) Amelia.

When the comedor was in sight, Evelyn said again, "I'm hungry!"

This time, however, she laughed and rubbed her belly. She loved coming to the comedor once the walk was over.

Other children were already there, but Catarina saw that no one was eating yet. Hermana Amelia stood outside, wiping flour from her hands and talking with Samuel, one of her helpers. Hermana Amelia seemed worried, and they both kept looking down the road.

That is when she noticed the girls. "Hola, Catarina! Hola, Evelyn! We are making the pupusas for you right now, but the water truck hasn't come yet." Pupusas is cornmeal mass stuffed with farmer's cheese, refried beans, or fried pork fat.

There were no faucets, sinks, hoses, or drinking fountains at the comedor. All the water they needed to cook food, to drink, and to clean up had to come by truck. Twice a week, a truck arrived carrying a large tank filled with water. But not this week.

Since the water truck had not come when it usually did, they had used up all the water they had received the last time. Hermana Amelia and her workers were not able to prepare food or clean the tables. It was very hot, and everyone was sweaty, hungry, and very, very thirsty.

Some children, like Evelyn, fretted and whined. Others played, but their play was subdued and slow. Catarina sat in the shade of the comedor with other girls, but they said little. The heat of the day made them sleepy. Nothing exciting or particularly happy was happening at the comedor today.

All that changed in an instant when Samuel announced, "Here comes the water truck!"

Whining children began shouting. Worried adults started laughing and came running. Those sitting on the ground jumped up to peer down the road. Children left their play and ran to meet the truck with the big tank of longed-for water.

"Get the buckets!" Samuel's voice bellowed over all the noise.

Everyone scattered to grab pails, jugs, and bowls—anything that would hold the precious water. The truck backed up slowly, and Catarina watched as a huge pipe came down from the water tank. From everywhere, children and adults came running and skidding in the dirt, nearly knocking each other down to reach the truck on time. They did not want to waste any water.

How excited they were as they heard the swoosh of the water rushing down the pipe.

A cheer went up as buckets were quickly placed under the pipe. Evelyn clapped her little hands and jumped up and down.

Catarina cupped her hand under the stream of water and drank some.

Samuel grinned at her and said, "Thank God for this water!"

Catarina noticed Hermana Amelia making a Sign of the Cross in a silent thank-you prayer.

Some of the bigger girls carried buckets of water on their heads to deliver it to the comedor. They laughed with delight when some of it splashed down onto their hot shoulders and arms.

Two small children struggled to carry one little bucket between them, giggling the whole time. Catarina lugged a pail, and Evelyn solemnly carried a bowl of water into the comedor. Samuel and other adults ran back and forth with buckets from the truck to the building and back again until all the water had been emptied from the truck.

The meal was then quickly prepared to the sound of song and giggles and much banging of spoons and cups.

Catarina, with Evelyn at her side, sat with the other children as Samuel led them all in a prayer. Their heads bowed, Catarina squeezed Evelyn's hand to remind her to keep silent.

It was quiet only for that moment, for the thankfulness they offered God in prayer spilled out like water from the pipe. The water had brought them life again, and it was time to laugh and celebrate.

A Light in the Darkness

A Story from Rwanda

DIRECTIONS: The child in this story experiences darkness in a very real, physical way, but she has also suffered many other forms of darkness in her young life. Light is beginning to come to her, again both physically and symbolically. Have the learners choose an art form such as painting or poetry to express the themes of darkness and light in this story.

INTRODUCTION: In 1994, a war in Rwanda killed one million people in only 100 days. Those who lived fled to refugee camps in other countries. Children who survived this violence had no opportunity to go to school while living in the camps. When the people returned home to Rwanda, these children, many of whom were orphans, were so far behind in school that they could not attend a regular school. In addition, they needed to work to provide food for themselves. With the help of UNICEF and the Rwandan Ministry of Education, classes have been set up for these children so they will eventually be able to attend regular school and make better lives for themselves.

Samara sat in the rickety chair, clutching a flashlight. Its beam pierced the darkness of the tiny place she called home, giving her a little comfort.

Night fell early in Rwanda, and every night now, Samara was all alone. Samara feared the darkness.

She had been a little child when a war had started in her country. Both her parents were killed early in the fighting. Samara, her grandmother, and her little sister fled to a refugee camp. Soon her sister became sick and died. Several years went by before Samara and her grandmother were able to return home. They moved back into the part of their house that was still standing. Shortly after they came back, Samara's grandmother died.

Now thirteen, Samara spent her days doing any work she could find and eating whenever she was lucky enough to get food. She could not read or write because she had never been to school. She knew she would never get a job that would pay enough for her to eat regularly and to fix her house. So she was alone in the darkness that was her life.

But tonight, Samara thought, was different. She played the flashlight over the walls and thought about what had happened earlier in the day.

Two women had come and told her of a new school that was starting for children like Samara. None of the students there could read or write because none of them had been to school before. Many were orphans like Samara. In this "catch up" school, Samara would meet other people. She would learn basic skills so she could eventually go to a regular school and have a meal each day.

Samara had listened, not believing this could really be true. Up until then her life had taught her not to hope. Yet, the two women offered her hope. She had learned not to count on anyone, yet the women claimed the school would open in the morning.

Always afraid to show her true feelings, Samara just nodded as the women spoke.

"You have no light in here," one woman observed. "And there are no street lights. It must get very dark here at night."

Samara could not keep the fear from showing in her eyes, but she remained silent.

"I have something that will help just a little," said the other woman. She pulled a flashlight out of her bag, along with a box of batteries, and handed them to Samara.

So now, Samara sat in the rickety chair, flashlight in hand, wondering what it would be like to go to school in the morning.

It seemed to her that the flashlight burned a little brighter, chasing away the darkness.

Glimpsing a Soul

A Story from Iraq

DIRECTIONS: Before the story share some of this information with the children, in addition to the Introduction.

Economic sanctions: when a country or a group of countries stops trade with another.

Trade: buying and selling between people or groups. A grocery store is a place of trade among those who produce the food, those who sell it, and those who buy it.

For certain reasons the United Nations placed economic sanctions on Iraq from 1990 until 2003. These were "full trade" sanctions, meaning that other countries could not sell anything to Iraq, and Iraq could not send out their products to be bought by others. However, in a country greatly damaged by the war and a corrupt government, those who were the most affected by the sanctions were not those in charge but families and children. With no trade, jobs were lost, and families became very poor. Schools and hospitals were damaged and could not be repaired because materials and equipment were not allowed into Iraq. Hundreds of thousands of children died as a result of these conditions. Those who survived did so only with great difficulty.

After the story use these questions for research and discussion.

- What are some of the effects of economic sanctions? Visit the Web site http://vitw.org/economic_sanctions for more information.

- What might be some alternatives to economic sanctions?

INTRODUCTION: Invasions, wars, and economic sanctions involving Iraq are very complicated and controversial issues. However, as these have had a tremendous effect on the children of Iraq, the readers of these stories ought to understand the circumstances of their Iraqi peers.

Unemployment in Iraq was as high as sixty percent in the year 2002, so many children, like Paimon and the shoe shiners, found ways to provide for themselves and even for their families, risking arrest and imprisonment. Paimon is a real child. The conditions under which she lived were the result of war and the economic sanctions that had been placed on Iraq.

The American woman named Lisa had arrived in Iraq just a few hours earlier. Her guide, Ramzi, was Lebanese-American, and he spoke Arabic. He had visited Iraq before and was telling her how changed he found the country. "It was such a lovely, civilized place. The people had a great interest in art, and Iraqi hospitality is amazing. But now, everyone has been so hurt by the corrupt government, the war, and the sanctions placed on them."

They looked around at a depressing sight of broken windows and poverty. Still, it was hard to think about anything but the intense heat. "It's well over 100 degrees, I'd guess," Ramzi said. "Over by our hotel we can stand in the shade and you can get your shoes cleaned."

Lisa agreed. After all the traveling she had done, her shoes were very dirty, and she did not want to be entering people's offices or homes wearing them as they were now. Still she was unhappy to see that the shoe shiners were young boys, whom she felt should be in school. As they headed across the street to the Al Fanar Hotel, an eleven-year-old girl came running toward them, calling out happily. She threw her arms around Ramzi.

"Paimon!" he exclaimed. "It's good to see you again!" Then he began speaking in Arabic to her. Lisa watched. Paimon was smiling up at Ramzi, her eyes shining. She seemed unaware of the searing heat, talking with great enthusiasm and moving constantly. Paimon, Lisa thought, was a bundle of energy.

But when Ramzi turned to introduce them to each other, Lisa saw that Paimon was more than friendly and energetic. Immediately she sensed

37

in Paimon something she could only describe as a glimpse of the child's soul. "She carries her own light," Lisa thought. "She is one of those rare people you meet briefly and never forget."

Still, her shoes had to be cleaned. When Lisa took them off, she gasped, "Ow! I can't stand on the pavement! It's too hot!" She began hopping from foot to foot.

Paimon gave a delighted laugh as she instantly slipped off her own plastic shoes. She placed them at Lisa's feet. As they were too small for Lisa, Paimon directed Lisa to stand on top of them. Lisa started to protest but Paimon insisted. Ramzi assured Lisa that Paimon really wanted her to use the shoes. Paimon jumped up and down to cope with the hot pavement, but she would have kept moving even if she had her shoes on. She was like a delicate butterfly, flitting from flower to flower.

Soon the shoes were cleaned, the boys were paid, and Lisa and Paimon were both wearing their own shoes again. Ramzi, Lisa, and Paimon walked together for a while. Paimon chatted with Ramzi, but she kept including Lisa by holding her hand and shining a dazzling smile at her. When they reached a street where they were to go their separate ways, Ramzi spoke again with Paimon and opened his backpack. He had a gift of honey from Lebanon for her family. Paimon hugged Ramzi tightly.

Then she turned to Lisa. Reaching into her pocket, Paimon took out an unopened box of chewing gum. She pried it open, shook out one square piece, and offered it to Lisa. "Thank you, Paimon!" Lisa said and they hugged. Paimon gave Lisa one last, deep look, then fluttered down the dusty, hot street. She turned to wave from time to time, and Lisa again thought of a butterfly.

Lisa turned to Ramzi, about to tell him how delighted she had been to meet such a wonderful child, when she saw a worried frown on his face. "Paimon just got out of jail," he said simply.

"Jail? Whatever for?" Lisa asked.

"She was arrested for begging on the streets. Paimon is the oldest of four children. The youngest is still a baby. You know, unemployment here is widespread. Paimon's father lost his job quite a while ago. He is a good man but devastated and depressed that he can't support his family, so he has left them. If I understood Paimon right, the father comes back from time to time, but it's up to Paimon and her mother to care for the family. So Paimon has taken to begging or selling things in the streets. She apparently brings in their only income that way. Unfortunately, begging is against the law. She was arrested once and spent a week in jail. Imagine an eleven-year-old in jail! But that was not all—she was arrested a second time and spent another week in jail. However, she has no choice but to continue. She was arrested a third time, this time for a month!"

They stood there silently, both gazing where they could still see Paimon far down the street.

Finally Lisa said, "Just for begging—just for trying to feed her family!"

Ramzi nodded. "Just for begging and selling gum."

Startled, Lisa looked down at her hand, where the little square of gum lay in her palm. This was Paimon's only means of income and she had freely and graciously given it to Lisa! Lisa looked up quickly, but Paimon had disappeared around the bend of the street.

To Love Tenderly

A Story from the Ukraine

DIRECTIONS: Family life comes in many forms. After reading the story, discuss with learners what elements make a group of people a family, no matter how they come together.

INTRODUCTION: This story is based on a true incident at a Ukrainian orphanage. While the Ukraine was under Communist rule, parents were urged to have large families. When Communism collapsed, so did the system of jobs. Many parents could no longer afford to feed their families. That and many other factors in a society in the midst of great change resulted in large numbers of children having to grow up in orphanages.

The teacher looked out the window of the orphanage classroom. Something was going on. She had sensed it during math class. Now she could see several children hurrying across the bleak yard called the playground.

They were not sauntering out to play football. The teacher saw destination and purpose in the intensity of the children's movements.

She decided to follow them. Some mischief-makers were with the group. She pulled on her boots, knowing she might encounter snakes. Slipping out the door, she followed, hidden from the children.

There was the usual mix of ages in this group. She loved the way the older kids looked out for the younger ones. If they couldn't have a normal home and family, at least they got a feel for what it meant to be brothers and sisters.

Now the group had quieted and was approaching a section of an old concrete pipe. The opening had been blocked with bricks and wood, and one of the girls was removing these.

Then the teacher heard a squeaky yelp and saw two puppies tumbling happily out of the large pipe! They were, no doubt, abandoned offspring of local wild dogs.

A delightful pandemonium broke loose as the children sprawled on the rough ground so the puppies could playfully leap onto them. She heard more puppy yelps and barks and shouts of glee and laughter from the kids. The teacher watched silently, appreciating the pure joy shared by the puppies and the children. The puppies were passed around, tenderly held, patted and caressed, tickled and scratched luxuriously.

Then the children began pulling bits of food out of their pockets, pieces of bread and other little things.

"Come on, Rex!" one of the little boys called, holding out a thin carrot. "Here you go—I saved it for you!"

They had food for the other dog (who was called Jake) as well.

One of the older children started cleaning out the sheltering pipe. Another produced some soft old clothing for a fresh bed.

The teacher watched, her fingertips pressed against her lips. She thought about how the children were taking such proper and tender care of the puppies—even though many of the children had not had the opportunity for the proper and tender care of parents. They gave what little they had—food from their adequate but not abundant meals and clothing from the supply closet.

And they were giving lavishly of their love.

"We'd better go in. It's getting dark," one of the older boys said.

The puppies were kissed and cuddled and fed more bits before being ushered back into the pipe. The bricks and wood were carefully replaced over the opening.

"There, no bigger animals will get to them," declared the boy holding the bricks.

"Good night, Jake! Good night, Rex!" one of the youngest children called out softly. "We'll be back in the morning!"

As the children trudged back to the building, the teacher stayed in the shadows. She did not want the children to see the tears streaming down her face.

A Plague of Locusts

A Story from Senegal

DIRECTIONS: This story presents a real and multifaceted problem in western Africa: a locust infestation. It shows the complexities faced by many people whose resources are always limited. Together locate the country of Senegal on a map. At least a dozen other countries have been affected. Locate some: Mauritania, Mali, Nigeria, Cape Verde Islands, Burkina Faso, Niger, and Chad.

Choose five readers for this story. Consider an adult for the narrator's part. After reading the story, help the students identify and list the problems presented in the story. Divide them into groups and give each group a copy of the following:

Your group is in charge of evaluating the issues and finding solutions. Choose one group member to take notes and give a report of your recommendations when you are finished. Consider these points in your discussion:

1. If the swarms are not controlled, the generations of locusts will destroy thousands of acres of crops and move on to other countries. Severe food shortages will result. Who could be responsible? List possible groups. Remember that you are considering a problem that affects many countries. Should countries that are not affected by the locusts work to solve this problem?

2. Not controlling the insects will cause great problems, particularly of hunger. However, widespread use of insecticides could easily cause other problems. What might they be? Are there any alternatives that will save crops and prevent hunger and still protect the environment for future growing seasons?

Gather as a large group to hear the recommendations from each small group. Conclude with a spontaneous prayer led by the learners.

INTRODUCTION: This story is based on real circumstances in western Africa.

Narrator   Welcome to Senegal. Our country is about the size of the state of South Dakota. You will find it pleasantly tropical here—warm but not too hot, and lots of breezes. We have three rivers, and of course, our western border is the Atlantic Ocean. We are blessed with more than five hundred and fifty animal species.

Our official language is French, but more that thirty dialects are also spoken here. Some industries are fish processing, petroleum refining, and phosphate mining, but most of our citizens farm. Peanuts, rice, corn, cotton, cassava, and groundnuts are our main crops.

We have many problems, however. Only forty percent of our children go to school. One-third of our adult population cannot read or write. Most of our farmers are subsistence farmers, which means they can barely grow enough food to feed their families. There is nothing left over to sell so they can buy other necessities.

Farmer 1   We already have very little to live on. If more problems arise, we have nothing extra to help us survive. We have had two years of drought, during which many of our cattle died and we often went hungry. Frequently we did not know where our next meal would come from. Then this year, we had a good growing season. Everyone was happier because the fields were green with life-giving plants. We planted food wherever we could.

Farmer 2   But before it was time to harvest, the skies turned dark with swarms of locusts. They descended on our trees, our homes, and of course, our crops. Millions and millions of crop-destroying locusts came—and came and came and came and came. It was a like a blizzard of yellow insects.

Farmer 3 I am the president of our local farmers' association. I'm here with the other members, fighting a losing battle with locusts. When the first swarms arrived, they ate a great deal, but not all, of our crops. Then they dug holes in the ground and laid eggs before they left here. Each female can lay as many as ninety eggs at a time, and each one lays eggs about three times in her lifetime. You can see thousands of holes. Soon the young will emerge. When they are young, they can't fly. We call them "hopper bands" at that stage. If we can't control them, they will eat everything we have left. Then they'll leave and go cause damage somewhere else.

Farmer 1 Unfortunately, the only way we have to control them is to dig trenches. When the hoppers come out of the holes, we will push them into the trenches with our hoes or brooms made of leafy twigs. They can't fly, so we dig the trenches deep enough so they can't jump out. Then we bury them.

But that's slow work and we can't destroy as many as we need to. If only we had insecticide! We're trained how to use it, but the people at the agriculture office keep telling us they've run out of it. We farmers are trying to buy some elsewhere, by having everyone in our villages give money. We have been told, too, that people in the rest of the world have been asked to contribute money so more insecticide can be brought in, but not enough money is being given. So, we keep digging trenches.

Army Colonel As the army commander in this area, I'm very concerned that the locust invasion will cause great suffering. Besides the people here, other countries have been hit, too. We hope to keep the locusts from moving on to even more countries.

We've trained a thousand soldiers to spray the affected areas and plan to train more. I send out teams to scout out the positions of new swarms. However, we don't have enough insecticide or trucks, so we are limited to small areas. But we are trying!

Large Farm Owner I'm the owner of a huge market garden. I employ several hundred people here and sell our produce in Europe. I have trucks, spraying equipment, and insecticide for my land, but these locusts have now become such a huge problem that I could still lose my whole crop. What's the point of planting? I have to decide soon, and what I decide will affect all my workers and their families.

Farmer 2 Two years of drought and now this! Look over there—there's a hopper band, eating the grass that my cows, sheep, and goats should eat. If I had enough spray to kill the hoppers, my animals would eat the grass that would be poisoned with insecticide. What then? If we drink the milk or eat the meat from the animals, will we be poisoned as well? And the river! The rain will wash the insecticide into it, and it too will be poisoned. Then what will my children drink if the river is poison?

To Belong

A Story from Romania

DIRECTIONS: After reading the story, explore the idea of one person's actions touching others. Talk about how the initiative on the part of Mark and Caroline Cook resulted in changing the lives of the children and all the new people who came to love them. See www.hopeandhomes.org for more information.

Discuss what kinds of changes your learners would like to make in the world. What would it take to make a dream become a reality?

INTRODUCTION: Romania is an Eastern European country that is beautiful and often sunny. It is also one of the poorest countries in Europe. Romania's people suffered for years under the rule of a dictator. Among the problems that resulted was that many children became orphaned. The government chose to place the children into large orphanages, where they were often neglected.

In 1994, a British couple, Colonel Mark Cook and his wife Caroline, became aware of the suffering of these children in Eastern Europe. They began an organization, Hope and Homes for Children (HHC), which works to "give hope to children worldwide who have nowhere to live, due to war or disaster, by providing them with loving family homes." HHC now works in six African countries and eight Eastern European countries, providing a variety of healthy and loving living situations as well as education.

In a farming village in Romania stood a large building, with patches of gray cement where the paint had chipped off. Electric wires hung down, dangling in the breeze. Many windows were broken. A tall fence circled the building.

Although the building housed an orphanage, no signs of children at play were seen, not even play equipment such as bicycles, balls, wagons, or swing sets.

Inside, the place was even less cheerful. All the walls had been painted an ugly brown to conceal dirt. No bright posters, drawings by children, or photographs decorated these walls. The air was filled with the smell of soiled diapers and wet blankets. Toys were nowhere to be seen.

The children were there—some half dressed, most underweight—looking out with vacant eyes. None of them ever had a chance for exercise or fresh air.

In one room, crowded with iron cribs, lay the babies. It was eerily quiet. No little ones were heard crying. Little Celi was among them. A blue-eyed baby, she had spent her whole young life in her crib. No mother's smiling face peeked over the crib at her when she woke. Only after she had wet her diaper many times and the bed sheets were wet did she get a clean diaper. In her short life, she had learned not to cry, for no one would come. Instead, she began rocking her head back and forth, back and forth. She made no attempt to sit. From time to time, she got eye infections, and often had lice in her hair.

Down the hall lived Andon. Though he was four years old, he had never left the main room. He had been in it since he was a baby. As far as he knew, the whole world was that room. He had not learned to talk. Often he sat in a corner, looking at his hands as he moved them in a pattern over and over. Other children were in the room, quiet like Andon, but he paid little attention to them.

One day several people came to the orphanage. They had arranged for better places for the children to live. Celi and Andon were the first to leave. Andon howled in fright, for he was leaving the room that was his world.

In her new house, tiny Celi rocked her head back and forth, staring into space and never crying. Her new, loving parents cleaned her up, fed her healthy food, and held her often. She was surrounded by intriguing toys, colorful pictures on the walls, and a soft and cuddly doll. Around her, too, were the new sounds of music and laughter. Little by little, her vacant look faded as she began studying her mother's face with great interest. Not long after that, she began to cry when she woke up from a nap because she knew someone would come to take care of her. And one bright day, she smiled. Celi was on her way to understanding what it means to belong to loving parents.

Down the street, Andon now lived in a yellow house. He had two parents and three older brothers. At first he sat in the corner, staring at his hands.

"Come on, Andon!" one brother invited. "Play ball with me!"

"Come on, Andon!" another said, grabbing his hand. "Let's go outside."

Frightened by these noisy boys who never seemed to stop moving, for awhile Andon retreated further into the corner. Plenty of love, good food, a warm bed with a soft blanket, and a happy family gave him courage.

Little by little, Andon stopped moving his hands in the familiar pattern. Instead he began using his hands to build with blocks, draw pictures, slide down a slide, and pull a wagon. Now the once silent little boy is the first to shout, "Good morning!" as he wakes up to yet another amazing day with his new family.

Just before Dawn

A Story from South Africa

DIRECTIONS: Have learners write about what they hope and pray for, and compare it to Beverly's prayers. They do not have to share this with others, but ask them to reflect on what they have written.

INTRODUCTION: AIDS is an illness found all over the world, bringing tremendous sadness and problems everywhere. However, countries that already struggle with great poverty often have much bigger challenges from AIDS than those with more resources. One problem is how to help the millions of children who are orphaned because of AIDS. In 2005, one estimate showed 1,200,000 orphans just in one country, South Africa. This story shows how certain organizations and neighbors work together to help children whose parents have died.

My name is Beverly. I am sixteen years old. I am both mother and father to my two younger brothers and my little sister.

Often at night, when they have finally fallen asleep, I sit by the window, looking out at the darkness. I cannot sleep because, like the others, I am hungry. I am also sad and very worried.

In the dark, I can remember the face of my dying father. "Take care of them," he had said to my mother. We could barely hear his voice, it was so weak. "They are good children and will need you to be both father and mother."

My mother had stroked his thin face and kissed his bony hands. Tears flowed down her cheeks and onto his.

That day he died.

He had had a sickness that scared people. They called it "AIDS." No neighbors helped us bury him.

In our sadness, we worked very hard so we could eat and I could go to school. My mother worked constantly, being both mother and father. At first I thought her tiredness and weight loss was because she was working so much. I did not want to believe that she, too, could have this terrible disease.

Then she started suffering from different sicknesses. As the months went by, she spent more and more time in bed. I left school to care for her and the younger children.

I held her head and spooned water into her mouth. "If only my mother were still alive," she whispered.

I knew what she was thinking. She wanted my grandmother to take care of us. In our country, aunts, uncles, grandparents and cousins lived nearby and helped each other. Because of our poverty and sicknesses, we now had a small family. I looked at my mother suffering and knew our family would soon be smaller.

So now, I often sit in the darkness, praying that I can find a way to keep us children together and not starve. Never mind school, clothes to replace our worn ones, or toys for the little ones. I just pray for food. I miss my mother's arms around me. I long for my father's warm smile.

Very early one morning, I heard someone call my name. I looked out our window. There was a neighbor, my mother's friend. She had been afraid to help my mother, afraid of her illness, but now she often left us some food. I was grateful. She had many children in her own home to feed.

"Beverly," she called softly in the gray of dawn, "some people from England have come to our town. I met them last night. They're helping children who are orphans. I told them about you. They want to help you and the little ones to stay together, and you will go to school again! You will learn a trade, and you will all have enough food!"

I stayed at the window after she left, thinking of my night prayers. I watched the sun rise steadily in the sky. A new day was coming.

44

To Believe Again

A Story from Sudan

DIRECTIONS: Those of us fortunate enough never to have been traumatized by war cannot completely understand its impact. However, trying to empathize is a small step toward peace-keeping. This story will help learners begin to empathize. Prayer is a natural response to empathy. Have your learners choose a prayer form (a novena, praying the St. Francis peace prayer, praying for children in certain countries, etc.) and use this for several sessions. Encourage them to continue praying at home for their traumatized peers across the world.

INTRODUCTION: The Republic of Sudan is the largest country on the African continent. It is slightly more than one-fourth the size of the United States. It has a long history and is home to at least thirteen major groups of peoples. Events in recent history have resulted in tremendous problems: a twenty-year civil war that caused the deaths of two million people, a large number of refugees flocking in from other countries, and bad weather for crops and food production. "To Believe Again" presents the situation of a boy who found himself caught up in these problems but who also looks with courage toward the future.

I thought it was a dream. I woke up, certain I had dreamed of the sounds of gunfire, for I often had nightmares. But the sound was very real. When I opened my eyes, I saw the worst thing a child can ever see: both of my parents lying dead on the floor.

I had also heard my brother's screams. Frantically I looked around for him, but I could not find him. I feared he, too, had been killed. I knew at that moment that I must run away if I were to live.

I ran and ran for days. I slept where I could, ate if I had food. I was always hungry, covered with bug bites, cuts, and scratches. I was dirty and scared. And lonely. So lonely.

I lost track of the days and weeks. What did it matter? After a long time, some people helped me. I was taken to a home with a loving family. I could keep clean and had a place to sleep. I felt safer. The people were good to me, and I was very grateful for the daily food. But still, I was lonely. I missed my family.

Then one day, I was told my brother had been found alive! I didn't believe it. I was afraid to believe it. Losing my parents and home made me afraid to believe anything.

Soon my brother walked in. We ran to each other and hugged and laughed and cried. Then we hugged and laughed and cried some more. We didn't want to let go of each other!

Today we live together here in this good home. I have begun to look to the future now. The sad and frightening memories will never go away. The loss of my parents will always remain a pain in my heart.

But my brother and I are together, and together we will make a new life.

A Prayer in Two Voices

A Story from the United States

DIRECTIONS: To achieve the effect of two voices, choose at least two readers for this story, preferably an older learner to read the part of Fr. Mike. To vary voices you may want more than one reader to take the parts of Kate and Father Mike. You might also have different persons read the lines for Ruth and Toby.

INTRODUCTION: The children in this story are fictional characters based on information from Father Mike Schwarte, who works for the diocese of Juneau, Alaska. Father Mike's work, explained in this story, is sustained by donations to the Catholic Extension Society, the largest supporter of Catholic missionary work in the United States. Visit **www.catholicextension.org** for more information.

Kate

My name is Kate, and I live in Hoonah, a fishing village in the southeastern part of Alaska. About eight hundred people live here. It is October, so it's starting to get dark now when I walk home from school. The long winter darkness is returning a little more each day.

Every day, though, I stop to look up into the mountains that surround Hoonah. Today was windy, and it drove a mist into my face, but I still stopped. I love the mountains. I feel lucky to live here.

My home stands in a long row of houses. All of the houses face the ocean. My dad loves that. He loves the ocean and mountains. I guess I'm like him. He usually supports us by fishing, but now it's deer season so he's hunting.

Dad loves living this way, changing with the seasons, working outdoors. But my mom doesn't like it. She keeps telling him that it's foolish to depend on the old ways, the ways of their grandparents. Whenever Dad goes away to fish or hunt, Mom becomes depressed.

Usually that's a pretty bad thing for us, and today was no different. When I pushed open the back door, a stale smell met my nose. I knew just where and how I would find my mom: asleep on the couch, an empty alcohol bottle on the table.

I sat down next to her, hoping she'd know I was close by. I noticed the lines of sadness around her eyes. After a few minutes, I could tell Mom wouldn't wake for hours. There was no point sitting there.

I went into the bedroom I share with Ruth, my sixteen-year-old sister. She was curled up on her bed, her ears encased in earphones. Music and marijuana were taking her far away from our life here. Ruth didn't care whether I was home or not, either.

I didn't hear Toby anywhere, so I went out to the kitchen. Through the window I saw my seven-year-old brother. He was happily splashing in a puddle, his open raincoat flying after him, his hair matted down with all the mist in the air. I suppose I should have called him in, told him to stop playing in the puddles. But he was having a good time, and I knew it was better for him than being inside with Mom and Ruth.

As I looked for something to eat, I noticed the calendar on the fridge. Yes! Tonight was religious education night! Father Mike's class! My day suddenly became a lot better.

Father Mike

Welcome to the diocese of Juneau, Alaska! It is one hundred miles wide and five hundred miles long. There are over eleven thousand miles of coastline, which includes islands.

I divide my time between two parishes and one mission town. I also work with children and teens. The towns are spread so far apart here that I had to learn to fly a plane. I take my Cessna 182 single-engine plane from place to place. I bring the Eucharist to the Catholic families in small towns. I try to bring encouragement and education, too. Sometimes I bring other things.

Often I ask people if they need anything. Prices are lower in the city of Juneau than out in the towns, so when I go down to Juneau, I get sacks of sugar or flour and other groceries for the people. On Mother's Day, I brought up a bunch of carnations and doughnuts for the kids to give to their moms.

Kate

I made a few sandwiches and called Toby in. He was excited when he realized it was, as he says, "A Father Mikey Mike night!" I didn't have too much trouble getting him to dry off and clean up. I had to run to keep up with him on our way to the church.

The lights were on in the community room, spilling an inviting warmth out into the night. As soon as we opened the door, Toby shouted, "Father Mikey Mike! We're here! It's me, Toby! And Kate!"

I was so embarrassed I wanted to run right back out the door. All the kids laughed, but Father Mike said, "Great! Class wouldn't be the same without you." I decided I could deal with the embarrassment.

It was a good evening, as usual. We laughed, sang, talked, and prayed together.

Back at home, I realized Ruth must have gone out with friends. Probably she had decided not to do any homework. I put Toby to bed. He never even asked about Mom. She had moved from the couch to her bed. But it didn't get me down. I lay in my bed, the quilt pulled up to my chin, and thought about the stuff we had talked about in class.

I kept turning something over and over in my mind. It was one of the things Father Mike said. He told us, "No matter who you are, no matter what your age or what you look like, whether you are rich or poor, you are important to God. God loves you. You are worth loving!"

Father Mike

I absolutely love being a priest. Sometimes, when I am flying, I really feel like the luckiest man in the world. I am able to do God's work! And when I fly, I can look down on God's beautiful creation—this is God's cathedral! I say a lot of rosaries when I'm up in the plane. I just hang the rosary on the handle and go to it! Of course, my parishes aren't like most of the ones in the lower states that have whole staffs. I am the priest, liturgist, and religious education director. I also take the money to the bank and lock the church doors!

Kate

The darkness is upon us now that it's December, but at school we've been busy working on a totem pole. It's good to have a project like this in the winter. It's almost finished, and by next week, it will be put up outside our school. My parents are coming for that. Toby can hardly wait.

Our school teaches us the language of our people, the Tlingets. We also hear the myths and stories that have been handed down from generation to generation. I have always loved these things. Ruth did, too, when she was younger, like Toby.

I am also learning a dance of the Tlinget people. There's to be a big celebration in Juneau and we are going to perform the dance there. When I went to practice, I was surprised to see Ruth there. I didn't think she would want to have anything to do with this, but she practiced hard, and signed up for a dance costume.

We walked home together.

"I went to talk to Father Mike," she told me.

I remained silent, waiting.

"We talked about the marijuana and about my grades. I'm having a hard time with studying. I just don't care. But Father Mike told me that God cares. God loves me, a pot-smoking, class-flunking kid! Father Mike helped me see that maybe God has a plan for my life."

I listened, hearing a new tone in her voice.

"Kate, maybe there's something important I'm supposed to do with my life! Did you ever think of that?"

She wasn't asking me. She was asking herself and her eyes had the faraway look. But it was not the marijuana-faraway look. This one was filled with hope and excitement.

Father Mike

The winters are tough here, and people are very isolated. Many adults become depressed, and some turn to drugs. Some of the adults also suffer from racism. In the 1940s through the 1960s, the schools in Alaska were either white or Indian. If a white person married a Tlinget Native, the children were considered "half-breed," a terribly racist term, and none of the schools wanted them. For the kids and grandkids, all this can lead to feelings of inferiority and trouble believing they are lovable. My most important work with the kids is to tell them that God loves them and so do I. I try to do things for them, like cheering them on in a game or going for a walk with them when I give retreats. Some kids call me, and we talk on the phone. I just try to be there for them and show them God's great love. I encourage them in their schoolwork, so they can begin thinking about having a great future, too. Of course, no matter how healthy or unhealthy a family is, they can have good times. There's not much to do here, so whole families often go out together, fishing, picnicking, or hiking. Not having a lot to do means they turn to each other. And that can be a beautiful thing.

Kate

It is June now, and sunlight is all around us, for months! Ruth, Toby, and I are at Camp Fun in the Sun, which Father Mike sponsors each year. Kids come from all over the diocese of Juneau.

My parents were surprised and happy when Ruth announced she wanted to go to camp. But I knew that Ruth is praying now, and she is looking for challenging things to do. Father Mike asked her to come to camp as a teacher.

When we first arrived, Toby was shy. I didn't know he had a shy bone in his body, but I guess he had never seen so many kids together before. He hid behind me.

Then we heard a familiar voice. "Who do I see over there?"

Toby lost all his shyness. He shouted, "Father Mikey Mike! Hi, Father Mikey Mike! It's me, Toby! Kate and even Ruth are here!"

Father Mike came over to us. "Great," he said. "Camp wouldn't be the same without you. I'm so glad you came!"

Toby jumped up and down. Ruth looked around for other kids her age who would be teaching, too. And I stood there in the midst of all the noise and excitement. How glad I was that I came, too.

The First Day

A Story from Afghanistan

DIRECTIONS: Consider the obstacles and problems the Afghan people have faced for several decades. Compare their problems to what you have faced. Discuss what our lives might be like if our country had suffered the same injustices and natural disasters.

Zakira's family is Muslim. If you would like to learn about a Muslim woman whose life is very different from that of Zakira's mother, check out the Web site **www.rukhsanakhan.com**. Rukhsana is Canadian-Pakistani and the author of many books and articles, as well as a public speaker and writing teacher. Her Web site offers a variety of topics for people of all ages.

INTRODUCTION: For twenty-three years, the country of Afghanistan has been plagued by drought, occupation by other countries, war, earthquakes, and terrorism. All this has affected the everyday lives of the people in numerous ways. One is education. Most of the people of an entire generation were unable to attend school. More recently, girls in particular were denied education. But with the help of Catholic Relief Services, community-based Accelerated Learning Programs are being established in rural areas. Since 2003, more than 2,000 children and women have received a primary education. Younger children are enrolled in regular schools. Even the preschoolers are in classes, taught by women who have benefited from the accelerated programs. These changes are bringing hope and enthusiasm to the communities.

Zakira's mother knelt in front of her and adjusted her white headscarf. "There, you are ready for this important day!" she said. She looked so beautiful when she smiled, and Zakira could see the love shining in her mother's eyes.

"Your first day of school is one to remember," her mother said, dressing four-year-old Jilla. "I will always remember my first day, too."

Zakira said, "Tell me about it!" She loved to hear her mother tell her stories.

Her mother looked at her, startled. "Today is my first day as well!"

"What do you mean?" Zakira asked.

"I've never been to school. All my life our country has had so many problems, I was not able to go to school. My brothers and sisters couldn't go either. But now, that's changing. I am going to school for the first time today, just like you!"

She took Jilla's hand. "Let's go!"

They stepped out into the sunshine. "Are you going to my school?" Zakira asked. "And is Jilla going to school with us?"

"No, Jilla has her own school. We'll go there first."

They soon reached the house of a woman named Aziza. She was at her door, saying good-bye to her daughter, Momina.

"What a wonderful day this is!" Aziza exclaimed. "A first day for many women! Can Momina walk to school with Zakira?"

"Of course," said Zakira's mother.

The two girls smiled at each other. Going to school with a friend! What a day!

"Come in and get Jilla settled," Aziza said. Jilla clung to her mother.

Zakira had been to this house many times, so she was surprised to see the changes. Now the front room was hung with pictures and posters for young children. There were books and toys, too. Three other little children were already playing.

"My mother is a kindergarten teacher now," Momina said proudly. "First she took classes to learn to read, then she took a special class to become a teacher!"

Jilla, who had left her mother's side, was happily paging through books. Aziza wished them all a good first day.

Zakira walked with her friend and her mother. Outside a small building, they stopped. Girls were hurrying in. Zakira's mother said, "Here we are! My school is a little way from here. Study hard, listen to your teacher, and be thankful you can go to school! I will see you at home."

Zakira and Momina took hands and shyly went into the building. A blue rug was spread on the floor, and the other girls were settling themselves on it. The teacher was a woman who looked happy to see so many students. Zakira and Momina sat down next to each other as the teacher began handing out notebooks. They smiled at each other. School had really begun!

Later that day, Zakira's family had gathered together in their home.

"We started working on reading already!" Zakira said. "The teacher said learning to read is like getting a ticket to go anywhere in the world! You can learn just about anything if you can read! And at recess, I jumped rope with Momina, and we made friends with two other girls!"

Jilla hopped up from her mother's lap. "I can sing a new song!" she said. "I can count, see? One-two-three-four! My teacher read us a story, too!"

Zakira's parents smiled at each other. "And how was your first day of school?" her father asked her mother.

"Wonderful! So wonderful! I've always longed to go to school! I've begun to learn to read also! There are so many things to learn—so much to understand! Zakira's teacher is right. I feel like I have a ticket to see the whole world! The teacher said that many women, after completing the accelerated school, are able to begin jobs."

"Like Momina's mother?" Zakira asked.

"My teacher?" Jilla asked.

"Yes," laughed their mother.

Her father said, "I don't know what makes me happier—that our daughters can go to school, or that you finally have the chance to go! I am very proud of all of you!"

Her mother looked at him and then at her daughters with her beautiful smile. And again, Zakira saw all the love shining in her mother's eyes.

A Place to Sleep

A Story from Sudan

DIRECTIONS: Invite the students to write about the thing(s) they are afraid of. Ask them to think about what would make them feel safer. If they wish, they can share what they wrote.

INTRODUCTION: Fighting in Sudan has forced Sudanese citizens to flee their villages. Even when they are at home, the danger of attack comes frequently. This true story is based on an incident cited in the book *No Room at the Table: Earth's Most Vulnerable Children* (Orbis Books, 2003). The author, Donald H. Dunson, has graciously allowed many of his experiences to be written as fictionalized stories in this book.

The American priest had come to war-torn Sudan. It was late and very dark when he arrived in this county so different from his own. Still, he was welcomed warmly by his host, the local priest.

It was not yet dawn when they walked over to the church for early Mass. His host unlocked the door, and they stepped into the dark, still church.

Out of the corner of his eye, he thought he saw a shadow move. Yes—a shadowy but small figure was nearby and had moved.

Then, all around him he sensed slight movements, and more and more small figures rose up from the floor of the church.

His eyes now accustomed to the dark space, he could see that the shadows were actually children. They seemed to be gathering up possessions, mostly sleeping mats. Bigger children helped little ones as they began to file toward the door. He watched, realizing there were at least one hundred children.

Some smiled and greeted the priests. Others, especially the youngest ones, were so sleepy they remained silent.

As the last child slipped through the door, the visitor turned questioningly toward his friend.

"They are village children, and most of them sleep here. This has been going on for months now. The church building is the safest place in the village. Parents have their children sleep here, where hopefully they will be safe from any conflicts during the night. Now they go home to start their day. Many have to walk several miles."

The American priest looked out the door to watch the sleepy figures, little victims of war, streaming out into the dawn to face another day of uncertainty and fear.

Would they all return safely tonight?

Following the Star

A Story from Bosnia

DIRECTIONS: Discuss where people are currently fleeing war. Talk about the Holy Family's experience of being refugees. Compose a prayer to the Holy Family to watch over the many refugee families in the world.

INTRODUCTION: After the fall of Communism in 1989, civil war broke out in the country of Yugoslavia. Different ethnic groups in the former Communist country wanted to gain independence. The result was fierce fighting, often based on ethnic differences, and many people suffered and died.

Every night was the same now that there was a war. Andrija and his parents would lie down on the mattresses and blankets on the floor in the living room and try to sleep.

Every night, the sound of gunfire was even louder than during the day. Andrija wanted to shut out the noise, and so he would plead, "Tell me a story, please, Mama?"

She would pause and say into the darkness, "What do you want to hear tonight?"

Every night she told a story, embroidering it with many details so Andrija could picture it in his mind. Then she would sing softly until he was finally asleep. He did not hear his parents' frightened whispers then.

Andrija was a young child, so he didn't realize how his father struggled to get them food and water regularly. He didn't notice the fear in his mother's eyes as she rubbed her abdomen where a brother or sister grew. He didn't pay attention when they talked of bridges and buildings being blown up.

But he did see war through his own eyes. War meant that no children could play outside. He longed to run in the park and shout and jump. He missed the sunshine. He longed to see the stars at night. "Stay away from the windows!" his mother would frantically call whenever he went into the rooms with windows, trying to peer outside.

War meant that sometimes he was hungry. He might eat potatoes often, but never chocolate, and he rarely drank milk. Sometimes they had electricity and sometimes they didn't. Even when they had it, they could not turn on a light at night.

War meant not being able to get a puppy. His father had said maybe someday, after the war. But Andrija longed for a puppy now.

At night the war seemed to come closer to Andrija. Every night he needed his mother's stories of places far away and long ago, where life was safe.

Months passed this way. Andrija began noticing it was darker and colder than before. One night, curled up close to his parents for warmth, he asked suddenly, "Is Christmas coming?"

"Yes," said his father.

"Will we go to Aunt Magda's house on Christmas Eve? Will we have lots of good food and go to church?" he asked, remembering the fun of last Christmas.

"No, I'm afraid not. It's too dangerous to go to Magda's house, and there is not enough food for a feast. Besides, our church is damaged. The walls are crumbling because there is a great hole in the roof."

Andrija lay quietly, not able to shut out the sounds of gunfire.

"But I can tell you the Christmas story," his mother said. "Long, long ago, a young woman named Mary and her husband, Joseph, were expecting a baby…"

"Just like us?" Andrija asked.

"Just like us," his mother said. "It was time for the baby to be born, but Mary and Joseph had to travel to another town…."

Every night he huddled under the covers and asked for the Christmas story. He fell asleep to dreams of shepherds and wooly sheep, of a baby in the hay, and a very bright star.

One day he played on the floor with his small wooden animals. It was hard to move them because he was wearing mittens in the chilly apartment. His father had gone out earlier, and his mother paced the floor as she always did when he left.

When Andrija's father came home, he brought no food. Instead, he held papers. "I finally managed to arrange everything!" he said.

Andrija looked up, startled by the hope in his father's voice.

"We leave tonight," his father went on.

His mother closed her eyes and whispered a prayer.

Andrija stopped moving his wooden sheep. "Where are we going?"

"Far away, to the countryside, to your grandmother's house. We should be safer there."

That night, he sat in a truck with his parents and other people. Andrija looked from face to face. Some seemed sad, others frightened. Everyone looked weary. There was one woman, bent with age, who kept muttering and looking at his mother. Andrija edged closer to his father, but he listened to her words.

"Christmas Eve and here we are, fleeing war. Some peace on earth! And a baby coming. Just like Mary and Joseph...poor child...."

Andrija turned to his mother and whispered, "Is it Christmas Eve?"

She nodded. He turned to the window.

"Look, Mama!" he shouted. He had to shout this time. "It's the Christmas star! See it?"

The others all smiled now, exchanging glances. Softly, a man began singing a Christmas song. One by one, the others joined him.

Andrija stayed at the window, watching as the battered city was left behind. The star remained in the sky, leading them to safety on Christmas Eve.

A Fair Life

A Story from Nicaragua

DIRECTIONS: Invite the learners to look up Fair Trade products offered through Catholic Relief Services (www.crs.org). Learn about products other than coffee that are sold through Fair Trade, and other information about this program.

Discuss: How do you think Mercedes' family might be living if they had not begun to sell their coffee through a Fair Trade program? How do you think your choices in coffee and other products affect people in other parts of the world?

Most of the Fair Trade products are grown without the use of dangerous chemicals, which means they are safer for those who buy them. It also means there is less damage to the environment, which benefits everyone. Research to find out what the difference is environmentally when coffee is grown in the sun and when it is grown in the shade. Find out why there are two ways and which is better and healthier.

INTRODUCTION: Despite their hard work coffee farmers are usually greatly underpaid. For a three dollar cup of latte, the farmer may make less than two cents. This means, of course, that for the most part coffee farming families are very poor. Because coffee grows only in certain climates, coffee farms are located close to one another. If all these poor families are in the same area, the result is an impoverished community. Education, health care, water systems, and other community services suffer, and in turn affect the families.

"A Fair Life" introduces the concept of Fair Trade and depicts the improvements in the lives of a coffee-growing family after they were able to join a Fair Trade organization.

Mercedes sat in the quiet of her family's small, dirt-floored house. In her arms, she held her one-year-old brother Carlos, who was sleeping peacefully. Despite the apparent serenity, she was too aware of the emotions of the others to feel calm.

Harvest time was ending. This should have been a time to celebrate a feeling of plenty. Instead, her parents hunched over their record books in the flickering candlelight, figuring out the family's resources for the coming year. They owned a small coffee farm. Though they all worked hard, they never received a fair price for their harvests. This year, they had been paid only eight cents for every pound of coffee. That was not enough to cover the costs of growing the coffee, much less provide anything else.

Her father's forehead was wrinkled with worry. Her mother's eyes betrayed her concern. Abuelo, her grandfather, shifted uneasily in his chair. His back ached but the medicine that helped him was not often available in the town store. When Mercedes looked at her father's face, she knew they probably did not have money for the medicine anyway. She was twelve years old and understood her father's great love for his own father. Not to be able to provide medicine for him must be so very hard.

But for now, she was waiting, as were her other brothers, eight-year-old Diego and fifteen-year-old Martin. "I don't know how we can buy the school uniforms and books," Mama said finally.

There, now it was said. Diego quietly went off to bed. Martin gazed out the window. There were no streetlights, only darkness. It was as if he were looking out at his future. Mercedes knew that Martin wanted to work the farm, to hand it on to the next generation, but they would be fortunate if they made it through the coming year.

In bed, Mercedes heard the snores of Abuelo and the soft sounds of Carlos sucking his thumb. She was listening to her parents' conversation. She heard determination in her mother's voice. "Every time I see my friends in town, they are talking about this Fair Trade movement. It sounds like a good way for us to do business. I want to start going to the meetings."

"Why not?" her father said. He sounded weary. "What do we have left to lose?"

Five years later, seventeen-year-old Mercedes walked home from town with six-year-old

Carlos. She carried a small box of groceries and Abuelo's medicine. Carlos clutched his brand new school uniform.

He was very excited about starting school soon. "I'm big enough to go to school with Diego now!" he said proudly. "I will study hard like you and Martin did!"

Mercedes smiled. "And you are well enough to go to school now," she added.

Carlos frowned. "Yes. I used to be sick a lot! Why?"

"Mama thinks it was the dirt floor in our house. All of us walking on the same dirt every-day made the dirt get so fine it became like a dust that got into our lungs. And you, being the small-est, would often get sick because of it. But since we put in the cement floor, you've been much better. We are all healthier and stronger because we have more food now."

They were walking along a paved road. "This road used to be all bumpy and muddy!" Carlos said. "Oh, look—I see another well being dug!"

Mercedes smiled at him. Carlos was always noticing things and then telling his family what he observed. They stopped to watch the well dig-ging. "More water for more people," Carlos said solemnly. Then as they neared home, Carlos announced, "There are a lot of birds. Martin told me there didn't used to be so many birds."

Before Mercedes could reply, Diego came run-ning to meet them. "Guess what! I heard Papa just say that next year, he thinks we can put in electricity!"

Mercedes gasped. Electricity! She could hardly imagine her little home with lights!

Later that day, Mercedes, Mama, and Carlos were sorting the green and imperfect coffee beans from good, red, ripe ones. Mama was humming a song. Mercedes looked at her healthy brother, and then to the coffee plants under the tall trees where Papa, Martin, Abuelo, and Diego were working. She ran her hand through the beans, knowing they would bring her family a decent income this year.

Carlos picked up one good bean. "We have a real floor." He picked up another one. "We have more food now." Holding up several beans, he said, "Diego and I can go to school and we can walk there on a good road." He scooped up a handful and said, "We are going to get lights. Abuelo doesn't say his back hurts. Mama, you sing now, and Mercedes, you smile more!"

Mercedes couldn't help but smile again.

Another Day like Yesterday

A Story from the Ivory Coast

DIRECTIONS: Before reading this story, give learners the definition and other information on child labor (see page 119). One area where child labor is sometimes used is chocolate production, the topic of this story. See Catholic Relief Services (www.catholicrelief.org) for information on Fair Trade chocolate as well as chocolate for sale.

INTRODUCTION: Chocolate is a favorite food of many people. Its basic ingredient is cocoa beans, which are grown in several countries. Child labor is often used in cocoa farming.

Growing cocoa beans does not pay well. Cocoa farming families are often very poor, no matter how hard they work. Some parents cannot afford to pay other adults to work with them, so their own children must help. Because these children miss school and the work is dangerous, this work is considered child labor.

Children are involved in cocoa farming in other ways. They leave their desperately poor families in hopes of being paid for jobs on cocoa farms. Instead they are tricked into working for no money and are not allowed to leave. This is considered slavery. The following story is about a child slave in the chocolate industry.

Each day was like the day before. Tomorrow would be just the same. Kontie could not imagine any changes.

A year ago, he had been living with his family in Mali. They were very poor, and there was never enough food for everyone. When a man came to their village and spoke of hiring boys to work on his cocoa farm, Kontie's parents listened.

"I see how you suffer here with so little," the man had said. "And I have a solution for you. Allow your sons to come with me to the Ivory Coast. There we have cocoa farms. The boys will be given good, honest work, and their wages will be sent home to you."

His parents not only listened, but also gave permission for Kontie to go with the man.

At age eleven, he went off to work, wondering what life would be like far from his village, the only place he had ever known. He was glad to be able to help his parents. He knew that soon the money he earned would be sent home.

Now he was twelve, and Kontie knew that no money was sent to his home, for he was never paid. He didn't expect ever to see his family again. All he'd learned about life outside of his village was life as a child laborer, where each day was the same.

He and the other boy workers harvested cocoa pods that grew near the top of the tree. This meant using sharp, long-handled machetes. The job was dangerous, and Kontie had seen more than one boy badly cut because of an accident with the machete.

Sometimes they sprayed the trees with pesticide. They were given no gloves or masks, so they got the pesticide on their skin and breathed it into their lungs, too.

Another job was to split the pods open—that was hard work! Then they scooped out the beans inside each pod and spread them out to dry.

Kontie heard that it took 400 pods to make one pound of chocolate, not that he knew what that meant. After all, he had never tasted chocolate.

The boys worked all day until 6:30 in the evening. Kontie and the others were exhausted and very hungry, but there was never enough food. And he had left home for this?

But Kontie couldn't leave the cocoa farm. He had no idea how to get home and had no way of contacting his family. Besides, he had seen a couple of boys who had tried to escape. They had been badly beaten. No, he would stay here and harvest beans for that chocolate stuff.

He walked back from the field to the building where he and the other boys slept. He heard the familiar sound of the key turning, locking them in for the night.

Today had been the same as yesterday. It would be the same tomorrow.

Something More than Fear

A Story from Sudan

DIRECTIONS: To better understand the main character's situation, have learners think about the previous day, listing (privately) what emotions they felt at differing times. After reading the story, have them write a short reflection on how they might feel if they were in the character's circumstance.

INTRODUCTION: Civil war in Sudan has forced many families to live in the crowded conditions of refugee camps, where they are crammed very close to one another and are plagued by fear, hunger, and boredom.

"Watch the baby and the others," Kaltoum's mother had said before she left the refugee camp. "I'll be back soon."

"Mama," Kaltoum started to say, but stopped when she looked into her mother's eyes. They both knew her mother was taking a great risk leaving the camp to collect firewood. Other mothers on the same task had come back badly hurt. Soldiers were often outside the camp, too, and they would beat any woman who left the camp. Kaltoum's father could not go because he would be shot.

Kaltoum turned her frightened eyes away from her mother. They had to have firewood, or the food they had been given could not be cooked. "I will take care of them, Mama," she said quietly.

The baby slept, since Mama had just fed him. But the other children were restless. There was so little space to play in this crowded place, no animal or garden chores to do, as they would have at home. They didn't even have a house. They slept in a structure made of plastic sheeting wound around poles.

Kaltoum gazed out onto the sea of plastic sheeting. She realized that she was often hungry, often scared, and often bored, but she no longer had any other feelings. She had stopped crying for all those she knew who had died. She couldn't cry forever, so she buried the grief deep inside of her. She never felt interested or excited anymore. When was the last time she had laughed?

Fatima, who was only four, began to whine and ask for Mama. Kaltoum shook herself. She had to put away her fear to help the others. With a forced cheerfulness, she said, "Fatima, let's sing a song. Let's see how many songs we know!"

Kaltoum cradled Fatima and sang. Their brothers sat nearby, half listening, half watching for Mama. Fatima fell asleep, and Kaltoum bent over to lay her down by the baby.

When she stood up, she saw Mama coming, a load of sticks carried expertly on top of her head. She was smiling.

Kaltoum smiled with relief. Mama placed the wood on the ground. She spoke quietly, so as not to wake the little ones. "I have just learned that they are opening two schools in the camp! You three can go back to school now! There are no desks, nor enough books, but there are teachers in camp anxious to get back to work. Somehow, they will teach you your Islamic studies again. And they hope to teach mathematics, science, geography, and English!"

Kaltoum felt something familiar. Excitement? Was that it?

She looked at her mother. Their eyes met. Right now, Kaltoum didn't feel fear, but hope.

A Chorus of War

A Story from Many Countries

DIRECTIONS: Choose four readers: a narrator, and readers 1, 2, and 3. Make certain that the readers are familiar with the names they will be pronouncing.

Narrator — Right now, more than 300,000 children are fighting in armed conflict as soldiers in more than thirty countries worldwide. Most of them were taken by force from their families, and they can be as young as eight years old.

Reader 1 — I am a child, but I no longer have the spirit of a child.

Reader 2 — I am a child, but I no longer think like a child.

Reader 3 — I am a child, but I no longer love like a child.

Reader 1 — My childhood was stolen from me. I was taken away from my family and forced to become a soldier.

Reader 2 — My childhood was stolen from me. After I was taken from my family, I was given a new name, Strike Commando. I was taught to act according to my new name, that is, to lash out at others as soldiers do.

Reader 3 — My childhood was stolen from me. As a child, I was taught to hate what I had loved. I was taught to obey only the adult soldiers. No one else matters, not even my family or friends. They would be afraid of me now, for I am a soldier.

Narrator — The child soldiers are used as front-line fighters, spies, messengers, and also to plant or clear out highly-explosive land mines.

Reader 1 — I am a child soldier from Sierra Leone.

Reader 2 — I am a child soldier from Cambodia.

Reader 3 — I am from Pakistan.

Reader 1 — Burundi.

Reader 2 — Colombia.

Reader 3 — Democratic Republic of Congo.

Reader 1 — El Salvador.

Reader 2 — Guatemala.

Reader 3 — Angola.

Reader 1 — Eritrea.

Reader 2 — Ethiopia.

Reader 3 — Rwanda.

Reader 1 — Sudan.

Reader 2 — Afghanistan.

Reader 3 — Liberia.

Reader 1 — Uganda.

Reader 2 — We are child soldiers who want to be children.

Reader 3 — Please, pray for us.

A Small Act of Friendship

A Story from El Salvador

DIRECTIONS: Natural disasters always cause suffering and many problems no matter where they hit in the world. Help learners see, however, that a place already impoverished and then struck with a disaster is much more vulnerable than a wealthier place. Poverty can mean problems with immediate rescue work, medical care, and subsequent rebuilding. Discuss the meaning of the Catholic social teaching, "an option for the poor and vulnerable," and how this story helps show the need for this principle.

INTRODUCTION: In January 2001, a devastating earthquake rocked El Salvador. A month later, a second one hit. More than 1,000 people died. Over a million were left homeless and without the basic necessities of food, water, and medical care. Aid workers rushed in, first with emergency relief help, then to assist in rebuilding. The following is a true story of the meaning that small gestures of caring have between people who face despair and suffering.

The truck bumped and rattled along the rutted road, carrying emergency supplies. The visitor peered out the window at all the damage two major earthquakes had done to a small, poor country. Houses and other buildings were just piles of rubble now. Fruit trees lay on their sides, and carefully tended gardens and farm fields were destroyed. It all seemed hopeless.

The visitor knew that the human suffering could not be measured. Hundreds of people had died in the earthquake. Those who had survived had no access to water or food. Still, he was unprepared for the sights that met him when the truck arrived at its destination.

Several hundred people were waiting for the supplies. Some looked dazed, as if they could not yet understand their loss. Others clearly wore their grief on their faces. Exhaustion and bewilderment seemed to be everywhere. Fear filled the eyes of so many people. Everyone was suffering from hunger.

Lines quickly formed as dinners of chicken and rice were distributed. The visitor noticed three young children coming down the hillside together. He saw their father direct them to go get food, but he did not come with them.

His wife had died when their house collapsed during the earthquake.

The visitor looked up at the father. As their eyes met, the visitor could see the struggle in the father's face. This unhappy man was not certain whether he wanted to live or die. His life, his love, and his hope had collapsed, just as his house had.

The father's look of complete despair frightened the visitor. He felt he must do something, however small. He decided to stand in line and get food for the father.

Hungry people looked at him questioningly. Why was this stranger, obviously not hungry, trying to eat the food he had brought for them? The visitor was embarrassed, but he stayed in line, wanting to show this father that someone cared.

After receiving the food, the visitor climbed the hill to where the father still stood. The visitor reached out, offering him the food. Again their eyes met. The look that had so frightened the visitor was no longer as strong.

That small act of friendship helped the father realize he could begin to hope once again, for he knew someone cared. He would eat so he could live and take care of his children.

One Thousand Bricks a Day

A Story from Nepal

DIRECTIONS: As you read this story, pause at the points where times of the day are mentioned. Ask listeners to think about what they are usually doing at those times. Invite your learners to act out or illustrate the story.

INTRODUCTION: Throughout much of the world, bricks are made by hand—often by children's hands. Brick making is a low-paying job, yet workers are expected to make hundreds of thousands of bricks in a year. Poor families have no choice than to have their children work with the parents. The work is extremely hard and dangerous and leaves no time or energy for the children to go to school. Some of the countries where children make bricks are Peru, Argentina, Ecuador, Pakistan, India, and Nepal. This story is about a family of brick makers in Nepal.

Safel was the youngest in his family. He was six years old. Six days a week, he worked with his sisters, Ambu and Banhi, his brothers, Kaushik and Daman, and their parents. Here is a typical workday.

4 AM

"Wake up, Safel," his mother calls. "You too, Banhi! Everyone else is up. If you want to eat, you must get up now!"

Safel rolled over. He was so tired. It was still dark outside, and he wanted to pretend it was night. His body ached from yesterday's work, and the work the day before that. But, he stood up and pulled on his work clothes. He and Banhi sleepily joined the rest of the family who were already eating.

In a short time, they were all on their way to work as the faintest light of dawn appeared in the sky. Daman carried the sack of food that would be their other meal that day.

5 AM

While their parents walked farther to another field, Safel and his siblings went into the field where they had worked yesterday. They began digging up the mud. The mud was thick and heavy, so Safel had a hard time lifting his shovel. He admired how quickly Daman and Kaushik filled their buckets. Safel and Banhi dug near each other, filling one bucket together and taking turns carrying it to Ambu.

Ambu mixed and kneaded the mud so it was the right texture for bricks. Then she lined up the brick molds and sprinkled them with sand. This kept the mud from sticking to the molds. Next she took the mud she had mixed and scooped it into the molds. When each mold was filled, she ran a long stick over the tops, smoothing off any extra mud. Expertly, she flipped the molds, and newly formed bricks came out. She did this over and over again until there were many bricks laid out near her.

10 AM

Safel stopped digging mud and wiped his forehead. It was very hot now, and he longed for a drink of water. There was none nearby, so he tried not to think about it.

"Let's line these up," Ambu called.

That meant Safel could stop digging for the day. Now he helped Daman and Banhi carry the fresh bricks to the spot where others were drying in the sun. Rows and rows of bricks were partially dry, some completely dry. They lined up the new ones carefully in rows, while Ambu and Kaushik continued to mold more bricks. The dirt under Safel's bare feet was hot, and he was dizzy with hunger. He was glad when Daman announced it was time to meet their parents.

1 PM

The midday heat made it impossible to work. The family sat together in the shade and ate their meal. Safel's food was gone before his stomach felt full, but he was happy to drink some water. His back and feet hurt. He looked at his hands and found several new cuts. He lay down with his head in his mother's lap and closed his eyes.

3 PM

The next thing he knew, everyone was standing up and stretching. The air was a bit less hot, so it was time to go back to work.

Ambu and their father went to the kilns. These huge ovens baked the bricks that had dried in the sun. The bricks had to be baked or "fired" before they were finished. Safel watched them go, and he felt a little jealous. Working with the kilns was a very dangerous job, for a person could be badly burned. Near the kilns the air was much hotter than on the hottest day. Still, he wished he could stay with his father instead of hauling all the dried bricks to the kiln.

"Safel, come on," his mother called. Reluctantly he followed. His mother was good at kiln work, but Safel knew she was hauling bricks so Ambu could learn to work the kilns. Their parents wanted her to learn this task because they were worried that all the brick carrying was affecting her growth. Ambu was too small for her age, and her back was a little bent, their father said.

Safel arrived at the stacks of dried bricks a few minutes after the others. He put his sack on the ground and began filling it with bricks. Then he hoisted it onto his back. He would carry the next batch on his head, just for a change. Slowly, weighed down by the bricks, he picked his way across the field, trying to avoid stepping on stones and broken bits of brick with his bare feet. He reached the site of the kilns and bent to set his bag on the ground.

"Safel!" His father's voice was sharp with worry. "You almost touched the kiln! Move away! And be more careful next time."

Safel walked back for another load of bricks. As he filled his sack, he heard Kaushik say, "I figured out that, on the days when we don't dig mud and mostly move bricks, we each carry about one thousand bricks a day!"

Kaushik was good with numbers.

Their mother looked up from the sack she was filling. "That's enough of that, Kaushik. What good does it do us to know that? I don't need to know how many bricks I've carried to know I'm tired. And what good does it do you to waste your time thinking of such things?"

"I didn't stop working to think about it, Mama," Kaushik said. "I just like to figure these things out."

"And where will that get you?" asked their mother sharply as she hoisted her burden onto her back.

The children stopped working, surprised by her tone. She sensed this and turned around.

"Get on with your work," she said more gently. The she smiled a little and said, "You haven't carried one thousand bricks yet today."

6 PM

They carried the last of the bricks to the kiln where Ambu and their father were emptying the kilns. This time Banhi got too close, and their father reprimanded her. Meanwhile Banhi was looking at a large burn on Ambu's arm that hadn't been there this morning.

Safel began piling the now-fired bricks into his sack. They were still hot, and he wore no gloves. He was careful not to drop any onto his bare feet.

Once again he began moving bricks, now to a place where they were stored until they were sold. He thought about the number Kaushik had said. He didn't know anything about counting, but that was probably a big number.

Everyone worked until it grew dark.

8 PM

Safel picked up the empty lunch sack and began walking home with his family. No one spoke. All Safel wanted now was some water and sleep. He knew there would be no food until the morning.

9 PM

Safel was sound asleep. Too soon, it would be morning. Too soon it would be time to make more bricks.

Blessings in the Dry Season

A Story from Tanzania

DIRECTIONS: Ask learners to devise an exercise at home that would give them the experience of meeting a basic need with great difficulty. Some suggestions: for a day, they must get their water from a faucet in the basement, or not use the stove or microwave and eat only cold food. Have them write a short reflection on their experience and share them in the next class meeting.

INTRODUCTION: Heifer International is an organization that works to end hunger and poverty in a variety of creative ways. To learn more about them, visit their Web site at **www.heifer.org**. In "Blessings in the Dry Season" we read about the difference that the gift of a donkey made for a family and a village in Tanzania.

Kulwa lived in a farming village in Tanzania. Not much had changed there in her twelve years. All of life evolved around two seasons: the season of plenty and the dry season.

Every year in December, someone in the village tapped into the trunk of the gnarled Black Water tree. Village families placed their buckets under the tap to gather refreshing water from it.

There was enough water for the villagers to drink, cook with, wash, and water their animals and gardens. This meant, too, that there was enough to eat. Mothers stayed in the village, tending gardens, cooking, and keeping watch over their children.

Then, every year in July, the Black Water tree ran dry. It would stay dry for six long months, and there was no other water source near the village. So each day, from July to December, all the village women walked twenty-four miles back and forth to get water. They carried the water home in buckets on their heads. This took them all day.

While they were gone, their children often went hungry. They were all thirsty, and it was hot and dusty. Some children would wander off. The children were always in danger of getting hurt while the adults were gone. Hungry and unsupervised, they did not usually attend school. Kulwa had

once been one of these wandering children. Now that she was older, she sometimes went for water, too. Usually, though, her mother wanted her to tend the house and care for her brothers. Kulwa kept her younger brothers safe, fed them what little cold food they had, gathered firewood, and did other chores. She did not go to school.

Kulwa knew all too well that during the dry season, the food in the garden barely grew. There was a limit to how much water her mother could carry for twelve miles, so there was never enough for the garden. This meant that food for the table was scarce.

Kulwa also knew that keeping clean leads to better health, but in the dry season water for regular bathing was scarce.

It was easy to get sick during the dry season. Every year it was the same.

Then, when Kulwa was thirteen, big changes took place. Missioners began a girls' high school a long distance from her village. Students would learn important job skills at the school. Kulwa's parents sold a cow so they could pay to enroll Kulwa. Up until now, Kulwa had experienced very few changes in her life, and she was nervous about leaving home. But if her parents believed so strongly in education that they made such a sacrifice, she knew she must be courageous. Kulwa left everything she knew, the good and the bad, and went away to school.

Kulwa learned and experienced more new things than she could count.

She returned home in the dry season. Despite all the changes she had gone through since she left, she expected the village to be the same as when she had left it.

Kulwa stopped and stared in wonder. The garden that was usually parched and struggling to grow was lush with large vines, and plants were heavy with vegetables. The garden was twice as big as it had been last year! The farm animals were fat and content.

She went into the house. Her mother was there. Kulwa had assumed she would be getting water. But there was water in the house, and her mother was cooking. Joyfully, Kulwa saw that her mother no longer looked so tired and thin.

Everything was clean and quiet. Her brothers were at school.

"How can it be so wonderful here during the dry season?" Kulwa asked. "What's happened?"

Smiling, her mother led Kulwa outside. Around the side of the house stood a gentle little donkey.

"There," her mother said. "That is what happened. We were given the gift of a donkey. I was selected to receive training on how to care for it, and then we were given the donkey."

Her mother went over to the animal and put her arms around its neck. "This faithful little friend can carry much more water than I can, so I no longer have to fetch water every day. And there is enough for the garden to grow well."

"The garden is bigger, too!" Kulwa said.

"Our friend helped me break the ground for the new section," her mother said, patting the donkey. "The donkey helps your brothers gather firewood, too. They can bring home so much more now. God is good, Kulwa. God sent people who help us and made creatures to work with us. And we return the favor by giving to others. My friend Suma finished her training just as this little donkey gave birth. We passed on the gift of that baby donkey to her. Now two households are richer."

Kulwa looked over at the garden and again at her mother. "Blessings, even in the dry season!" she said and reached out to hug her mother—and then the donkey!

Resurrection in Cape Town

A Story from South Africa

DIRECTIONS: Invite the learners to look up these words on the Internet or at a library: South Africa, apartheid, and "truth and reconciliation." This search will raise many issues that can be discussed in relation to Catholic social teachings.

You might have students write their own story about the woman's experience in this shantytown, or illustrate it in pictures.

INTRODUCTION: The vast and beautiful country of South Africa has many resources but also many problems. For centuries, outsiders came in to rule over the people, and their wealth led to an elitist government that kept people strictly separated, based on race. Severe repression and poverty were a result. Now, South Africa is experiencing an extraordinary healing process as the people work to bring justice to those most hurt by racial prejudice.

Some of the people, however, still suffer in poverty. "Resurrection in Cape Town" speaks about the human spirit and its ability to rise above poverty.

The city of Cape Town looks out over the waters where the Indian Ocean meets the Atlantic. A visitor from the United States marveled at the great beauty of mountains and the sea. She also enjoyed the warm welcome she received from many people.

Her work was to provide housing. One day she went to a shantytown to better understand the need for housing in the area. Shantytowns are unofficial neighborhoods with the houses of the poorest of the poor.

The woman stood quietly, taking in the whole sight. The houses were formed with everything imaginable. Any length of boards, sheets of plastic, old tires, wooden packing crates, cardboard of many shapes, and even an occasional window.

The shanties were small, of course, and built very close together. They almost seemed to hold each other up.

Two children came out of one shanty, school books in hand. The children smiled at her.

"Hi," she said. "Could you tell me why your houses are so close together?"

One child stopped to answer her. "The wind, of course. When the winds are strong, shanties built close together are more likely to stay standing," he said politely.

"Thank you," she said.

He gave her another beautiful smile and dashed off.

She wandered farther and came to a packing crate decorated with the drawing of a barber giving a haircut. Drawing closer, she could see that this packing crate was actually a barbershop, open for business that morning. Other crates were various stores.

All around her, children were following sandy paths on their way to school. The smell of simmering fish head soup drifted in the air. Mothers, carrying babies snuggled on their backs, were off to the one water faucet shared by all the residents. Little children too young for school scampered around their mothers at the water faucet. They stopped to wave at the visitor. She waved back, feeling that she had made friends without saying a word.

A man was approaching a shanty. He was carrying a window. He saw her watching.

"What luck!" he called. "I found not only a window frame but it still had most of the glass in it!"

The visitor, sensing she was welcome to watch, saw the man quickly take off several boards from his shanty to create a space for the window. He reused the boards to cover a space where the wall was made only of cardboard.

She did not know whether to cry at the poverty or to rejoice at the ingenuity of the shantytown residents.

A woman carrying a pail of water came and stood next to her.

"A window!" she exclaimed. "How wonderful! We'll have some light now!"

The man looked up from his work and smiled. "I knew you'd like it!" he said to her. Then to the visitor, he said, "This is my wife."

The visitor suddenly felt she was intruding. She was surprised when the woman invited her into the shanty. Once inside the visitor felt the same mixed feelings she had earlier. This home, held together by a few nails and a prayer, was one of extreme poverty. Yet a gaily colored curtain covered the door opening, a scrap of carpet lay on the bare ground, and everything was clean and neat.

"I thank you," the visitor said, "for making me so welcome in your home."

As she left, walking amid barbed wire fences and garbage, she was again greeted by the friendly children who had no toys or playground.

That night, far from the shantytown, she thought of the darkness that would seep into the shanties, where only a few paraffin lamps fought off the dangers of the night.

A few days later, the visitor heard that one of those lamps had fallen, starting a fire. The closeness of the shanties now worked against them. The fire spread rapidly from shanty to shanty. No one was hurt. No one was greatly shocked. Fires in a shantytown were nothing new.

But the visitor hurried back, fearful of what she would see.

From the ashes, the shantytown was rising again. Neighbors were there, sifting through the rubble, salvaging the wood that was not com- pletely charred. She saw the school-age children. One found a usable chair, another unearthed a cooking pot. The smell of soup was gone, replaced by a stench of spent fire and wet wood. A teenager was dragging a piece of plastic sheeting into the area, followed by a man carrying a packing crate.

Then the visitor saw what was left of the window, half buried under some broken boards, the frame and all the glass gone.

But no one was weeping. No one was enraged. And the little children still smiled and waved at her.

Living at the Bottom in the Mountains

A Story from Nepal

DIRECTIONS: After reading the story, encourage the learners to research and discuss:

- the origins of the caste system
- the typical marriage age in Nepal
- the education levels of people in the different castes.

INTRODUCTION: Situated in the Himalaya Mountains, the country of Nepal has eight of the ten highest mountains in the world. With rushing rivers, ice-blue lakes, and an area of flatland, Nepal is diverse and extraordinarily beautiful. However, in this land of highs and lows, the Nepalese people themselves are labeled as high or low. The caste system places people in upper classes, or castes, and lower castes. A person cannot ever change castes or marry someone from another caste. Persons in the lower castes, about twenty percent of the whole population, are considered dirty and "untouchable." This system keeps the untouchables from getting much education or good jobs, and they live in great poverty. There are several castes among the lower castes. The belief of danger by touching is so widespread that people of different lower castes will not touch one another. Though the caste system became illegal in 1990, it is still widespread.

The delicate colors of dawn were just beginning to touch the hamlet where fourteen-year-old Sundari lived. Her one-room clay house nestled closely among the other houses. Beyond them stretched the staggering heights of the world's highest mountains. In the dim light, Sundari let the chickens out and milked the goat before she heard the wails of her infant daughter.

She brought the goat's milk inside where her mother-in-law handed her the baby. Sundari set-tled down to feed her child. As she did so, she ate a small bowl of rice and thought of her husband. He had left just a few days ago for India. They both hoped he would find regular work. In the village he had sometimes been able to get work as a day laborer, cutting stone or working in the fields of the upper caste families. But his wages were paid in rice and lentils. They could not buy what they needed with lentils!

Many people in this situation were forced to borrow money, which led them into debt. They spent the rest of their lives trying to pay it off. Desperately hoping to avoid this, her husband left for India with high hopes. Sundari and the baby remained behind with his parents and younger brother.

Whether her husband got work or not, Sundari had to fetch the daily supply of water. She pulled the sling of fabric over her shoulder to carry her daughter and snuggled the baby into it. Sundari set off to the water taps, following the narrow path that wound uphill. Other women and young girls were there, taking turns using only one of the two water taps. Sundari took her place in line, singing a soft song to her baby.

Before her turn came, another woman arrived. Sundari recognized her as from an upper caste household. This woman climbed a little higher to where the water pipes divided to reach both taps. She turned off the water leading to the tap Sundari and the others used. No one protested as the water in their tap slowed to drips. Instead they watched as she climbed back down and turned on the other tap. The water flowed out quickly, much more quickly than the other tap had flowed. The woman filled her buckets and headed back down the hill. After she left, Sundari's neighbor climbed up to turn the water back on for their tap.

Sundari was not tempted to get the water from the other tap, for she knew that the god that watched over their village would become angry if unclean people such as Sundari took water from it. The god would then make people sick. Her mother always told her that if she took water from the wrong tap, the water source would dry up right away, and someone in her household would die. She never questioned this. It had always been that way.

Instead, she waited to use the same tap as the other lower caste women. Then, shifting the weight of the baby and water buckets for her trek down the hill, she set off. Gazing at the beauty of the mountains all around her, she admired the gardens near the big houses of the upper caste families. She knew her mother-in-law wished that they, too, could have a garden, but they had so little land. Besides, they could not carry enough water for a garden. The upper caste people had workers who could help with that.

As Sundari reached her home, her mother-in-law came out and took the heavy water cans from her. She was already cooking on the outside stove. Sundari thought of her own mother and wished she could see her. Then she rubbed her abdomen, wondering if perhaps she was carrying another child. Her mother-in-law looked at her thoughtfully and then went back to her cooking. She did not protest when Sundari sat down instead of starting a new task.

Sundari took the baby out of the sling and smiled as the little one crawled across the trampled ground near the house. The sunlight was stronger now, and she felt a gentle wind in her hair. Closing her eyes, she raised her face to the sun, enjoying the warmth for a moment. Then she stood to get on with the work of the day.

Simplicity on the Soccer Field

A Story from Guatemala and the United States

DIRECTIONS: Use this story, based on a true incident, to start discussions on ways to simplify living.

- Talk about personal experiences of this kind. Discuss whether complicating factors add to or subtract from an experience.
- Name ways in which having a large amount of material goods or numerous choices may actually take away from the pleasures in life.
- Challenge the learners to name ways in which they might simplify their own lives.

INTRODUCTION: Living can be very complicated, no matter who you are or where you live. In every life, however, some things can be done in simple, uncomplicated ways. We each need simplicity in our lives because simplicity can promote health, happiness, and a feeling of peace. It helps us see the beauty in God's gifts around us, gives us time to help others, be creative, pray, read, and have fun.

Scene 1: Guatemala

Tomas had just finished feeding the chickens when his friends Felipe and Marco came running. Like Tomas, they wore no shoes or shirts, just jeans.

Felipe held up a soccer ball. It was white and black, very dirty, and some of the leather was peeling off. The ball also needed to be inflated, but they had no way to do it. "Ready to play?" Felipe asked.

Tomas ran off with his friends to start a game.

Scene 2: United States

Tom was in his bedroom, rummaging through the clothes dumped on his bed. He wore his freshly-washed soccer jersey, but was trying to find his checked-green shorts and his soccer socks.

"Tom! Hurry up!" his father called. "The game is at six o'clock, and we're carpooling with Martin. We have to leave in five minutes! Traffic may be bad."

Tom threw two pairs of jeans, a sweatshirt, and three T-shirts onto the floor before he found the soccer clothing. Quickly he pulled on the shorts

and socks, grabbed his large black and green soccer bag and ran to the kitchen. There he snatched a water bottle from the refrigerator and went to the mudroom to collect his cleats and shin guards. He wanted his sandals, the ones that massaged his feet after he played a game, but he couldn't see them in the mess of shoes in the closet, and his father was honking the car horn impatiently. Tom shoved what he had into the bag and hurried out to the garage.

Scene 1: Guatemala

Tomas, Marco, and Felipe soon reached the place where they usually played, a field of patches of grass and patches of dirt. Some other boys quickly joined them, including two of Tomas' cousins. They chose sides. They needed goals, so the boys of one team found some rocks for one goal while others used sticks to form the second goal. Within seconds, the game began.

Scene 2: United States

When Tom's father pulled up to Martin's house, Martin came running outside, his large bag bumping against his hip. He jumped into the back seat.

"Cool bag!" Tom said.

"Thanks. I got it for my birthday. I also got new shin guards," Martin said, unzipping his bag and pulling out the guards. "They're form-fitting and the ankle guards come off."

Tom looked at the equipment with a little envy. He would like new shin guards, but he knew his parents had just spent over 200 dollars to get him a rebounder net for the backyard so he

68

could practice by himself. They wouldn't be able to get him new shin guards yet.

Tom's father and the boys arrived at the field a half-hour later, but most players of the other team had not yet arrived. Tom and Martin sat down on the benches to put on their cleats and shin guards.

"Oh, no, I forgot my goalkeeper gloves!" Martin moaned, rummaging through his bag.

"Coach will be mad," Tom predicted.

The two coaches were talking, but soon Tom's coach had his team doing warm-up exercises. Tom wondered if the game would start on time. Then he watched as Martin informed the coach that he had not brought the gloves. Poor Martin, he thought.

Scene 1: Guatemala

The game was still going. Marco had a little blood on his shin where an opponent had accidentally scratched him with his toenail, but they kept playing, shouting, and laughing.

Scene 2: United States

The game started ten minutes late, and both coaches seemed irritated at the late arrival of the other team. Whistles were blown, and the players were off, the plump white and black ball skimming over the grassy field.

Scene 1: Guatemala

The players took a break, playfully teasing each other. They decided to choose new teams and play another game.

Scene 2: United States

Parents were on the sidelines, making a lot of noise. Some were yelling encouragement, others shouting instructions as loudly as the coaches. Two parents were talking on cell phones but keeping their eyes on the field. Martin's mother arrived in her work clothing and had a hard time walking across the thick grass in her high heels.

Scene 1: Guatemala

Tomas was darting and dashing across the field when he felt the button on his jeans pop off. He scooped it up from the ground and realized his zipper had broken too. Tomas grabbed his pants by the waist to keep them up and sprinted over to another part of the field. The others kept playing.

Within seconds, Tomas found a length of string on the ground. He paused to thread it through the buttonhole and then through the lever on the broken zipper. He tied the string tightly. There. That would keep his jeans up. He rejoined the game.

Scene 2: United States

After some hard play and many directions from the coaches, the game ended. Tom's team had lost. He changed from his cleats to his other shoes, wishing he had been able to find his massaging sandals. As he sipped some water, he heard his father and Martin's mother discussing the next game.

"I'll be out of town, so I won't be able to drive them," his father said.

"I can never get out of work early enough," Martin's mother said. "I'll see if Martin's dad can come, but he's on call that day and when he's on call he never knows if he can make a commitment…"

Tom, irritated at the loss, sighed and waited impatiently. He hoped they would work it out. He didn't want to miss a game. He was hungry, too.

"Dad!" he called. "Can we go out for pizza?"

"No, I've got a meeting tonight. And we have to stop for gas on the way home. We almost didn't make it here."

"What about when you get home after your meeting? Couldn't we go then?"

"You have to be up early tomorrow—did you forget you have hockey tryouts?" He went back to working out rides with Martin's mother.

Martin, mad that they lost and even more mad that he had forgotten his goalkeeper gloves, sulked on the bench. Tom sat down near him, but neither spoke.

Scene 1: Guatemala

The evening was coming on when the boys slowed down and ended the game. They each had jobs to do at home. Tomas picked up the deflated soccer ball. Still laughing and teasing each other, they walked home on dusty feet.

A Locked Room at Journey's End

A Story from the Ukraine

DIRECTIONS: You might have your learners discuss what it's like to start in a new school or join a new group. Or find some passages in the gospel that apply to the story. You might also ask them to prepare a prayer service for children living in orphanages.

INTRODUCTION: After years under Communist rule, Ukraine once again became an independent nation in 1991. However, the country was left with enormous financial problems, and much rebuilding needed to be done. Many people suffered because they could not afford or could not obtain the most basic necessities. Parents of large families found it impossible to provide adequately for their children. Sometimes, one parent of a family left to seek jobs in other places. Some children were orphaned, others were abandoned. As a result, thousands of children were placed in orphanages. Today these orphanages are staffed with caring people but are short on most supplies and equipment.

Larissa had stopped watching out the train window. After almost ten hours of traveling, she had seen only mile after mile of open land. She had dozed and eaten her lunch. Now, as the journey was reaching its end, she felt fear and dread, feelings she had known so often when she lived with her grandmother.

Larissa's parents had died when she was young, leaving her grandparents to raise her. While her grandfather was alive, they had a good life together. He was kind, and they had gotten by with what they had. Larissa had started school like all the other children in her neighborhood in Kiev. But two years ago, her grandfather had died, and her grandmother, never a strong or happy woman, began drinking heavily. She no longer cooked or shopped, so Larissa was often hungry. Her grandmother expected Larissa to do all the cleaning and laundry. If she didn't do it to her grandmother's satisfaction, Larissa was beaten. Often she had to choose between doing schoolwork and housework. Fear of her grandmother made the choice easy.

Finally a teacher intervened. She noticed Larissa's declining schoolwork and the bruises on her body. Now Larissa was on her way to an orphanage where, she was assured, she would receive better care. She took a deep breath to try to calm herself, but it didn't help much.

Larissa was the only child coming from Kiev, but she would not be arriving at the orphanage alone. Also on the train were six young children who had boarded a few hours after Larissa had begun her journey. They had been in an orphanage since they were babies, but that orphanage only kept children up until the age of three. Now they needed to transfer to another place where they could stay until they were seventeen. These little ones, two girls and four boys, were leaving the only home they had ever known, and the scene at the train station had been a tearful one. Larissa was glad when they all fell asleep, hoping they would relax for a while.

When the train stopped, it seemed as if they were in the middle of nowhere. Larissa was relieved to see a woman waiting for them. Larissa helped the little ones tie their shoes and wipe their noses before they got off the train. Even though they had never met before, the children clung to her hands.

The woman on the platform smiled. "Larissa? Welcome. I am Veronika, the director of the orphanage. You are almost home—it's only fifteen more miles by car. I know you'll make many new friends there," she said. Then she squatted down and addressed each young child, sorting out their names and welcoming them.

Larissa helped Veronika settle five of the small children in the back seat. Little Sasha wrapped his arms tightly around Larissa's waist, so Veronika said Larissa could hold him in the front seat.

As she drove, Veronika said quietly to Larissa, "Whenever a new child arrives, we have to be careful about sickness. So for two weeks, before you join the other children, you will live in a separate room. We just need to be certain you are healthy. I'll explain this to the younger children when we get there."

Panic rose in Larissa. Two weeks by herself? "I know I am healthy. I feel fine!"

"That's good, but we don't know if on the train you were exposed to anything like chicken pox or strep throat. If you get sick and are with the other children, the disease would spread like fire in the orphanage. We simply don't have enough medicine to take care of it. We don't have any antibiotics at all. Plus, we don't know what vaccinations you've had, or if you might have something called HIV. So this is the best way," she said in a gentle voice. "The two weeks will go by quickly. Then you will eat with everyone in the cafeteria. You'll be assigned a bed with another girl until you are thirteen, and then you will have your own bed. You'll start school, too. I bet you'll enjoy that!"

"Is the school nearby?" Larissa asked. Her voice sounded very small.

"It's in the same building as the orphanage. You don't have far to go to the classrooms. In fact, some of the bedrooms are connected to a classroom," she said. Then she announced, "Here we are!"

They pulled up outside an old brick building. The paint on the wooden window frames was peeling. The building seemed large and gloomy against the open landscape. Only one swing set stood on a dirt playground. Larissa noticed two rather flat soccer balls lying in the dirt.

She got out of the car and began taking the assorted suitcases out of the trunk. The handle on one was broken, and she scratched her hand on it.

"Uh-oh!" said little Sasha.

"Oh, it's just a little scratch," Veronika said brightly. "We'll take care of that right away."

They entered the building where another woman met them. She took charge of the six small children and led them away to a room. Larissa followed Veronika into a small room with a bed and a chair.

"Here you are, for the next two weeks anyway," she said cheerfully. "Now let's see that scratch."

Larissa held out her hand. Veronika took a bottle from a shelf above the chair. It was an antiseptic, and Larissa saw with astonishment that it was bright blue. She now had a long, jagged blue line across her hand, which made the scratch look much worse than it was.

"Make yourself comfortable. I'll be back to check on you soon," Veronika said. She smiled at Larissa and then left, closing the door after her.

To Larissa's horror, she heard a key turn in the lock. She had never been locked into a place before. She would be a prisoner in this room for two weeks—or would it be two weeks? What if they kept her in this room forever?

She thought about her grandmother's quick temper and swift fist. She looked around this room and wondered which was worse.

Then she heard noise outside the room and looked up at the small window in the door. There were several children there, mostly about her age. All of them were waving and grinning at her! Were they making fun of her?

Tears welled up in Larissa's eyes, and she wanted to turn her back and ignore everything. However, the noise kept up and she looked again. One girl, not tall enough to see in the window, kept jumping up and down and giving a wave whenever she was up in the air. Then Larissa realized the others picked her up so the girl could really look in at Larissa. The girl gave her a big smile and pressed a piece of paper against the window. Larissa hurried over to the door to read it.

"Hi, Larissa! Let's be friends!" it said.

Larissa managed to smile back before the others put the girl down.

A bell rang, and a mad scramble began as everyone outside the door prepared to head to class. But they did not leave without giving Larissa more smiles and waves of welcome.

A Yellow Dress for Kalimall

A Story from India

DIRECTIONS: Discuss arguments against slavery. Invite your learners to retell the story in Kalimall's own words, or that of the father or mother.

INTRODUCTION: In many places in the world, people are forced to live as slaves. In India, if a very poor man needs money, a rich person may "loan" it to him. But then the lender (or creditor) sometimes makes the poor man work for him for years. If the poor man has children, they too must work for the rich person. Sometimes even the grandchildren work. They work for no money, have little to eat, and are not allowed to leave for school or play. Children born into this kind of slavery do not know what it means to be free. They are unhealthy because they are undernourished and they must work very hard. No one in the family can read or write, so they don't know about the laws that could protect them. They do not know how to defend themselves.

This kind of mistreatment of people is not legal in India, but it still happens. Fortunately, certain groups of people work to help free these families. "A Yellow Dress for Kalimall" shows what it meant to one family to gain their freedom.

Kalimall should have been in third grade, but she had never seen a school. She didn't know what a book was, or that other children her age could write and do math. She had never had a doll or other toys. Her clothes were dirty and tattered.

Very early every morning, she went with her brother and a cousin to the stone quarry. She worked with them there, breaking up huge stones with a hammer. If she didn't do this, she might be beaten by the boss, or his wife would hit her and deprive her of food.

Kalimall's mother, father, and grandfather did all the other work on the boss's large lands and house. They were as afraid of the boss as Kalimall was. The family was always hungry because they were not given enough food. The boss never paid them for their work, either.

Late one evening, Kalimall curled up on the floor, exhausted. She slept for a short while, but woke at the sound of voices. With sleepy eyes, she saw they had a visitor, a woman who spoke softly but encouragingly.

"Your boss is breaking the law by forcing you to stay here. Now that we have filled out these forms," she said to Kalimall's father, tapping some papers on her lap, "I will take you tomorrow to the magistrate. We'll begin the process of getting your freedom."

"No! I can't leave here or my family will suffer!" her father exclaimed.

"You will all go with me," the woman assured him.

The adults continued to talk. They so rarely had visitors, and never so late at night. Kalimall wondered what all this meant, but she was so tired, she couldn't stay awake to find out.

Long before dawn, her mother woke her. Kalimall was hungry and thirsty, but knew her mother must go to work before she could feed the family.

But this morning, her mother did not go to the boss's house. "We are leaving here," Mama said quietly. Kalimall wondered again what this talk about leaving meant.

The girl sat up. The strange woman was still there. "Hello, Kalimall!" she said cheerfully. "You will always remember this day! Get up now for we are in a hurry."

No one explained to the little girl where they were going, for everyone was nervous and had to hurry. Soon Kalimall was walking away from the boss's land with her family and the woman. The girl had been told to be very quiet. Everyone watched carefully for the boss or someone else who would stop them. But it was so early, they saw no one until they had reached the town.

Kalimall stared at the buildings and at all the other people in the streets. Looking at their shoes, then at her dusty bare feet, she followed her family into the building where the magistrate worked.

They all sat down in soft chairs in a waiting room. "I'll go now to arrange a court appearance for your freedom," the woman explained.

Kalimall looked at her grandfather. He had worked for the boss's family all his life. Did he know what this thing the woman called "freedom" meant? She sensed that he was nervous, but he winked at Kalimall. Still tired and sleepy, Kalimall leaned against him and dozed until the woman returned.

"Your case will be heard in a few days," she said. "So now, we need to find a place for you to stay, as well as some food and clothing."

Kalimall didn't understand that the judge at the court would decide if her family would be free, or if the boss had to pay them for the years they had worked for him. She didn't understand that her parents would need to find a way to make a living even though they could not read or write. She didn't realize that she would start school soon. She didn't know that she did not need to be afraid of the boss anymore.

But she did understand that things were going to change for the better for her family when the woman brought her a yellow dress with a lace collar.

After Mama helped Kalimall put the dress on, Mama buttoned it up in the back and combed Kalimall's hair. Then Kalimall turned around, and her mother inspected her. Mama's eyes were wet with tears.

Kalimall and Mama held hands and sang all the way to the courthouse.

Journal of an Amish Girl

A Story from the United States

DIRECTIONS: Have your learners separate into small groups and discuss these questions: What do you think it would be like not to have electricity, a telephone, a television, or a car? Why do you think people choose to live the Amish way in our modern world? The Amish religion affects the day-to-day life of its people greatly. Is that true for Catholics? How?

Ask them to share their answers with the other groups.

Invite them to write their own diary for a week, then share what they wrote.

INTRODUCTION: A Swiss Protestant group that began in 1693, the Old Order Amish now live in the United States and Canada. They believe that Jesus teaches people to live as sisters and brothers in peace. Consequently, they will not fight in wars, and they always help one another. The Amish closely follow rules they read in the Bible. They want to live very simply, so they choose not to own cars, tractors, computers, or televisions or to use electricity at all. They travel using horse and buggy or by walking, though they will take planes, trains, or buses, or a ride in a non-Amish person's car when there is an emergency or a very long distance to travel. Several families may share one telephone, used just for emergencies. The women make most of the clothing for their large families, and the clothing is very plain. They raise much of their own food. Our government has made special laws to protect the Amish people's religious freedom. One law states that Amish children only have to go to school until eighth grade.

In this story, the life of a twelve-year-old Amish girl is shared with us through her journal. Rebecca lives on a farm in Pennsylvania with her parents and eight siblings. She speaks three languages and calls her parents Mamm and Datt.

May 9

Today was a regular day. We got up at 5 AM and did the farm chores. After breakfast, we kids walked to school. Soon my sister Sarah and cousin Kathy will graduate from eighth grade. Then they'll be all done with school. I have one more year. At school we started with a Bible reading and prayer. I studied all my subjects: reading, arithmetic, spelling, grammar, penmanship, history, and geography. All eight grades are in one room, and everyone is Amish. There are four students in my grade.

May 19

One of our horses is sick. This is especially bad because we need all four horses in planting season. Uncle James is coming over to help. Datt says Uncle is particularly good with horses.

June 6

We are enjoying the first of the garden produce, the peas, greens, and radishes we planted in the spring. Today I worked with my sisters Sarah, Mary, and Susannah to plant the second batch of tomatoes. Tomorrow we put in the pumpkin and squash seeds. You can just see the feathery tops of the carrots now. The beans are growing nicely, too, and my littlest sister, Rachel, is excited because she planted those. Mamm says young children should plant beans because they come up so quickly, and so they see the "fruits of their labors" right away.

June 27

Aunt Emma and cousins spent the day with us, picking strawberries and making jam. Aunt Emma told Mamm she is expecting a baby. This child will be their seventh. I hope it is a girl; they already have five boys!

July 12

Today is hot but breezy. I love hanging the wash on the line when it's windy. My silly little brothers ran between the flapping sheets. Our parents are worried about Jacob, my older brother. Every Amish person decides for himself if he wants to be baptized, and it is Jacob's time to choose. This is a big decision, for it means you are forever Amish. Last year, a few young people decided not to be baptized, and two left our community. My oldest sister, Mary, chose to be baptized, but we don't know what Jacob will do.

August 16

This week was our turn to have the church service in our home. Our congregation has no church building, so every other week we have services in someone's house. Datt says that helps us remember the very first Amish who were persecuted and so met secretly in their homes. Mamm says it also helps us to see that our religion is our life. So yesterday, Sarah, Mary, Mamm, Aunt Emma, and I made food for 200 people—bread, jam, beets, pickles, cheese, dried apple pie, and "church spread" (peanut butter mixed with marshmallow—yum!). Then we cleaned the house while Datt and my brothers cleaned the barn. Some of the cousins, Daniel, Thomas, and Joseph, had come with Aunt Emma. The boys moved the furniture from the living and dining rooms into the bedrooms. (It was tricky climbing over that furniture to get into our beds!) When the bench wagon arrived, we set up the backless benches in the empty rooms. About 8:00 this morning,

everyone arrived. Jacob was in charge of putting all the horses into the barn, and my cousin Daniel helped him. Buggies were everywhere! We sat on the benches, men and women in separate rooms. We sang hymns for a half-hour, then the bishops and deacons preached. They're from our community. One is Uncle Amos. They preached two sermons, and the hourlong one was about not judging others. Then we had prayer and more singing. After the three-hour service, we ate, talked, and played until everybody left to go milk the cows. It's an honor to host the church service, but I'm tired!

September 6

Exciting news! First, Jacob announced he will be baptized. I could see how relieved Mamm was. Datt, in his quiet way, smiled too. And if that wasn't enough, Mary came home and David Yoder was with her. They told my parents they were engaged! Datt and Mamm are very happy tonight. We are all happy!

Shadows inside the House

A Story from around the World

DIRECTIONS: Research more about child domestic labor and the many efforts made to rescue children. The Lutheran Immigration and Refugee Service Web site, www.lirs.org, has information and links to other organizations that work to end this injustice. Other Web sites on this topic: www.globalmarch.org, www.bba.org.in, and www.youngworkers.org.

INTRODUCTION: Child labor takes numerous forms. In many places in the world, including the United States, children are forced to work as live-in domestic servants. Working for a family in their home, rarely allowed to go outside, denied schooling or friends, and often working as many as fifteen hours a day, these children are easily hidden from view. What happens to these "shadow children" can be extremely harsh.

Reader 1

Here I am, a girl from Nigeria living in a comfortable house in a suburb in the United States. Sounds nice, doesn't it? That's what I thought when an American woman visited my town. She told my parents and me that if I came to live with her, I could get an education in an American school. I was so excited! My parents were very happy! But when I got here, I was never enrolled in a school. Instead, I was forced to work as the woman's slave. I cook, I clean this house, and I take care of the woman's children. She hits me whenever she is not happy with my work. I think something must be wrong about keeping me here. Every time someone comes to the door, the woman sends me into the basement and says, "Stay there and do laundry until I call you." I think she is hiding me. I don't know anyone else in this whole country. I have never even met the neighbors. I can't contact my parents. I don't know what to do but I want to go back home!

Reader 2

I am a child servant in Indonesia. I work for a family with small children. Each day I spend about fourteen or fifteen hours doing chores, but at night, when the little ones wake up and cry, I must get up with them. No matter how long I am up at night with a sick child, I must still be ready to make breakfast early. I cook three meals a day, every day, wash all the clothes and iron them. I clean the house, too. If the little ones mess it up, I hurry to clean it up. And if a child falls and gets hurt, I know I will be blamed and I am very afraid.

Reader 3

I am a domestic servant in Haiti. I am eight years old. Besides cooking and cleaning up all the meals, I shop for the food. I like to go outside for that but I dare not stay to enjoy it because I will be beaten. I never know what the lady might use to hit me—a cord, a broom, a belt. Once, when I was ironing and accidentally burned the collar of a shirt, she hit me with the hot iron.

Reader 4

I am ten years old and have worked for a family in the Philippines since I was six. I work so many hours and the work is so hard that I am tired all the time. If I don't work fast enough I don't get food. That makes it harder for me to work because I am hungry and tired. My mind gets tired from being yelled at and being afraid of being hit or kicked. I'll tell you what all this does. When you're tired it is easier to make mistakes, like tripping and spilling hot tea, or cutting yourself with a sharp knife when you are cooking. Nobody cares. They don't clean your cuts or bandage your burns. Maybe instead they'll hit you. "You stupid! Look what you've done!" the man yells. Then I know he'll kick me or hit me with something. It's like a circle—I get so tired and hungry I make mistakes. Then they beat me and starve me, and I make more mistakes because I can't move very well. But so far, they have never put chains on me.

Christmas in January

A Story from the United States

DIRECTIONS: After learners have read about Orthodox Christmas symbols and celebrations, have them research to learn about Easter festivities.

INTRODUCTION: About one thousand years ago, the Catholic Church divided into two main groups. Today we call these groups the Roman Catholic Church (which is made up of both Eastern and Western Catholics) and the Orthodox Church. These groups hold many of the same beliefs, but also have some differences. Because the roots of these two churches run so deeply together, Roman Catholics should know something about Orthodox Christians.

This story introduces a few differences about when and how Christmas is celebrated in the two churches. Orthodox Christians observe Christmas on January 7. Why? It has to do with different calendars. Orthodox churches chose to keep what is called the Julian calendar for religious celebrations. The Gregorian calendar is what is mainly used throughout the world. There is a thirteen day difference between the two. Thus, Christmas Day for Orthodox Christians falls thirteen days after December 25.

By January 6, at Ellen's house the Christmas tree had been taken down. Life had settled into its normal routine after all the Christmas celebrations. Ellen had been invited to her friend's house to celebrate Christmas Eve. Katie was an Orthodox Christian, and her family celebrated Christmas on January 7. Ellen felt honored to be invited, but she was a little nervous.

She rang the doorbell and Katie opened the door. "Hi! Come in. You are just in time to help set the table," Katie said.

"Okay," Ellen said, pulling off her jacket. Nothing difficult about setting a table, she thought.

Katie led her to the dining room where a woman was unfolding a tablecloth. "Grandma, this is my friend Ellen," Katie said. "Ellen, my grandmother."

"Just in time to set the table!" Katie's grandmother said.

Ellen nodded and smiled politely, but wondered what the big deal was about setting the table. Then she noticed a box on a chair. The box was filled with straw. Katie and her grandmother took some of the straw and spread it on the tabletop. They placed additional straw on the floor under the table.

"We do this to remember that Jesus was born in a stable," Grandma explained. "Now let's do the tablecloths."

Ellen helped Katie and her grandmother lay a tablecloth over the straw on the table.

"Katrya," Grandma said, "get the other one now while I go get the kolach."

Ellen looked at Katie in bewilderment.

"Katrya is my name in Ukrainian. Grandma likes to call me that because I was named for her sister Katrya who still lives in Ukraine," Katie said.

Ellen nodded. "But why another tablecloth? This one already covers the table."

As they opened another folded cloth and placed it over the first one, Katie said, "One is for our ancestors. The other is for us."

As Ellen smoothed the top cloth, she thought of the tablecloth used at her house at Christmas. It was printed with angels and stars. It made her think about the Christmas story, but it did not have the kind of symbolic meaning these two cloths had.

Grandmother came in from the kitchen carrying beautiful bread on a tray. Ellen saw that the bread dough had been braided and formed into three circles. The three circles had been stacked on one another before baking.

"We call this bread a *kolach*," Grandma said when she noticed Ellen examining the bread. "We have three layers for the Holy Trinity—one each for the Father, the Son, and the Holy Spirit.

The bread is formed into a circle to show that God is forever."

"Because a circle has no end," Ellen added.

"Exactly. Now hurry, girls, and go outside!"

In minutes, Ellen was zipping up her jacket and standing just outside the front door with Katie. It was nearly dark. "So what are we doing out here?" she asked.

"Looking for the Star of Bethlehem," Katie said. She laughed when she saw Ellen's eyes widen. "Oh, come on! Don't you do things just because it's Christmas? Things that make Christmas so special?"

"Yes, I suppose we do. We hang stockings and mistletoe."

"Well, we look for the Star. There! The first star! Now, let's go in. I'm freezing!"

Back in the warm house, Katie's parents, grandmother, and older brother were near the table. Ellen greeted them and noticed that in addition to the plates and silverware in their usual places, an icon of Jesus had been placed in the center of the table.

Grandma held up a sheaf of wheat stalks. "We call this the *didukh*," she said. "We believe the spirits of all our ancestors live in the wheat during Christmas."

As Grandma reverently placed the wheat near the icon, Ellen thought of her own grandfather who had died earlier in the year. Her mother had placed a picture of him near the Christmas tree.

Katie's father placed a bowl on the table. "Ellen, this is called *kutia* or 'God's food.' It is boiled wheat, like a hot cereal, with poppy seeds and honey," he explained. "It is the most important food we have tonight."

Then he set the bread on the table and dipped it in honey as he prayed. When each person had a piece of bread, he exclaimed, "*Khrystos Razhdaietsia!* Christ is born!"

Everyone sat down to eat. Ellen learned there were twelve courses in honor of Christ's twelve apostles. After the kutia, they enjoyed beet soup, two kinds of dumplings, and stuffed cabbage. Then there were the fish dishes—baked, broiled, fried, in aspic, fish balls, and herring. The meal ended with *uzvar*, twelve fruits stewed together.

After the solemn meal was over, there was much laughter and talk. Ellen felt the joy she always felt with her own family at Christmas. She joined Katie's family as they sang Christmas carols.

She smiled at Katie and said, "Merry Christmas, Katrya!"

Katie laughed and answered, "Khrystos Razhdaietsia!"

The Playground

A Story from Sri Lanka

DIRECTIONS: Invite learners to draw their vision of the playground the Mercy Corps built. Discuss how playgrounds can be theraputic. How did playing affect them as young children?

Talk about what a tsunami is. Why does it do so much damage?

INTRODUCTION: On December 26, 2004, an undersea earthquake in the Indian Ocean caused a tsunami of such great proportions that it took the lives of nearly one-quarter of a million people. While several countries were affected, it is estimated that in Sri Lanka alone 30,000 people died. About 12,000 of them were children. The survivors' need for food, medical care, clean water, and shelter was staggering, but the response from the rest of the world has been heartening. Slowly, survivors and relief workers are healing and rebuilding. Housing, schools, and businesses are all being constructed, but children in particular have other needs after such an overwhelming tragedy. The following story is based on a true story of people coming together in Sri Lanka to address these needs. Workers with Mercy Corps (**www.mercycorps.org**) spent one day using salvaged materials to build a playground for children living in a camp. The experience was a joyful one for all involved.

The little girl in the green dress watched a truck pull up in the camp. Ten adults got out of it, laughing and teasing each other as they unloaded cans of paint, tools, and ropes.

She didn't know what they were doing there, but then everything was hard to understand. Ever since the Big Water, she didn't know what to expect. She clearly remembered her village, her home, their animals, and her father's fishing boat. And she remembered her mother and her brother. But the Big Water had taken all that away, and life was hard to understand now. She watched everything but didn't ask questions.

So now she studied these newcomers and their many cans of paint. Her father and other adults came out of their makeshift houses and greeted the people who had just arrived. Her father showed them the piles of things he and others had collected: palm tree trunks that had fallen, a large collection of coconut husks, some old tires, and a heap of cans. The villagers and the people from the truck talked and pointed all around as they looked over the large, open space near the camp. Together they began dragging the heavy tree trunks to different places, fetching paint cans and coconut husks, and choosing tools. Then everyone got to work. What were they doing? A building that could be used for a school and a meeting hall had already been built. Puzzled, the girl watched as the group dug holes, groaned, laughed, and strained to make several tree trunks stand up straight and in place. These trunks formed a square. The group attached ropes from one trunk to another. After that, a man began painting the trunks a cheerful orange. The girl knew that the space marked off by the trees was too open for a house. And it wasn't a stable because the ropes were too high to keep any animals in.

But then she noticed other activities equally puzzling. The pile of brown coconut husks was getting smaller as one person painted each one and set them to dry in the sun. They were red, blue, green, yellow, and orange. The little girl loved the colors. Still, this was strange. She had always seen coconut husks, but she had never before seen anyone paint them!

Her father and another man were climbing one of the trees that had survived the Big Water. They brought a long, thick rope up into the tree with them. She moved closer to listen.

"Children's parks are a very important part of life here in Sri Lanka," her father was explaining to the newcomer. "The park nearby where I grew up was my favorite place in the whole world when I was a child!" She could see that he was smiling. She hadn't seen him smile for a long time. "It is important that the children here have a park, too. They have lost so much—much more than anyone should ever have to lose. They need to play again."

"Yes," the stranger agreed, unwinding part of the rope coil. "Play will help them heal. They need to laugh and imagine again."

They tied the rope securely into the tree and let the rest of the rope slip down. The end came close to the ground and swung gently back and forth.

As they climbed down, the little girl turned and noticed that someone had attached the colorful coconut husks to a tree trunk, the whole length of the trunk. Each one was a little distance from the other. Then they put it firmly into a hole into the ground, making it stand up straight, and securing it so it would not fall down. She gazed at this strange tree that had no leaves on top, but many-colored coconut husks on the trunk. Now they looked a little like steps. Well, whatever it was, she liked it!

Other members of the group had been busy creating things as well. Now there was a row of short sticks standing upright in the ground, with hoops to throw over them. Some old tires had been painted green and hung in a way that she recognized as swings. One narrow tree trunk lay on its side, but it was on a base someone built, so it was a few feet off the ground. Two women were painting it, and one said, "This will make a great balance beam!"

The sun was going down when all the workers stood back to admire their work. They were hot and tired but full of good spirits. Then there came a shout. The rest of the camp children had arrived.

"A playground! A playground!" they shouted.

Instantly there were two girls teetering on the balance beam. The long rope her father had hung was swinging madly with several children clinging to it and shrieking with delight. Little ones climbed happily onto the green tire swings. The girl realized the strange open structure was a jungle gym.

She watched all this with great dark eyes and listened to the happy shouts and giggles and laughter. She didn't notice her father until he took her hand and led her to the tree with the red, blue, green, yellow, and orange husks. He showed her how to put her feet on the bottom husks and use the others to climb the tree. She quickly scampered to the top. She paused and looked out over the camp and at the new playground. Then looking down she saw the happy, loving face of her father. She laughed and waved to him.

Carrie's Circle of Courage

A Story from the United States

DIRECTIONS: With your learners brainstorm for New Testament stories that are examples of courage, generosity, respect, or wisdom. Discuss how these attributes can help bring about social justice.

Help learners research the Lakota people's history. What are some of the lessons Carrie learned at St. Joseph's?

INTRODUCTION: Carrie is a girl of the Lakota Native American culture who learns how to practice some of the values of her people. While the story and characters are fictional, the school, St. Joseph's Indian School, is a real place in Chamberlain, South Dakota. It is a residential/educational facility for Lakota (Sioux) children and youth, and an apostolate of the Congregation of the Priests of the Sacred Heart. Their mission is to provide Lakota children with a living and learning environment that responds to the needs of the whole person, developing skills necessary to live a balanced and healthy life. You can find out more about St. Joseph's by visiting its Web site at **www.StJo.org**.

Carrie is twelve years old. Her grandmother is her guardian as her parents are not able to care for her properly. When Grandma became sick, she decided to send Carrie to St. Joseph's School, where her granddaughter could have a home as well as a school. We will read about a few experiences Carrie had during her first school year there.

Autumn

Carrie looked shyly around the living room where she had gathered with the other girls. She was the only new girl who lived in this house, and tonight she would learn just what the school year would bring. Mike and Susan, her houseparents, came from the kitchen carrying popcorn and juice.

"Welcome back, everyone!" Susan said cheerfully. She looked, Carrie thought, as if she really meant that. "And a special first-time welcome to you, Carrie! Have some popcorn, and we'll tell you a little about us."

"Such as who always leaves her dirty socks under her bed, right, Lara?" a girl named Jenna teased.

Everyone laughed, including Lara, who wiggled her stocking-covered toes at everyone.

"And how about who makes the best chocolate chip cookies?" Mike asked, smiling. Then he went on, "We'll discuss house rules and the job list tonight, too. Homework time will be from 6:30 to 8:00 like last year, after sports practice and dinner."

Carrie's stomach churned with worry. Usually she loved popcorn, but she was too nervous to eat right now. Would she get a lot of homework? She had never done too well in school and rarely did homework. And what if she didn't know how to do the house jobs? She could barely pay attention until Susan talked of being Lakota. Carrie had always known she was Lakota. Grandma spoke of this often.

Lara was answering Susan's question. "The Circle of Courage helps us understand the way we Lakota people try to live. The circle is made up of courage, generosity, respect, and wisdom."

Winter

Carrie showed a great deal of courage as she plunged into life at St. Joseph's. She played basketball, something she had never tried before, and she skated, something she had always loved doing. She made friends, especially with Jenna. Though she struggled with reading and math, Carrie found that, with help, she could do them. And she loved science class! Carrie also learned to work with Lakota beadwork and was preparing a gift for her grandmother as the snow and winds swept across the Dakota prairie.

When Carrie's thirteenth birthday arrived, she could smell the birthday cake in the oven. She heard Lara and Susan in the kitchen cooking her birthday dinner. But Carrie also enjoyed having some time to herself. A package had arrived from her grandmother, and she wanted to be alone when she opened the gift. In the package she found a light blue sweater, warm and wonderfully soft. Carrie knew her grandmother had knit it herself. She ran her hand lovingly over it.

"Carrie!" Her roommate Jenna stood in the doorway. "That's beautiful! Would you hold it up, please?"

As Carrie held up the sweater, she saw delight in Jenna's eyes. Jenna had warm clothes because the school provided them, but she did not own anything as special as this. "Try it on," Carrie offered. She watched Jenna admiring it in the mirror. Lakota people strive to be generous, Susan had often said. Carrie had frequently seen her grandmother give away something she had just baked or knit. Susan also said, "Love your neighbor as yourself, as Jesus taught." Carrie decided to speak with Susan or Mike about giving her new sweater to Jenna for Christmas.

Spring

The bus bumped along as Carrie and several other students rode to the reservation one day. They entered the cafeteria where many Lakota elders ate lunch each day. It was not long before Carrie found herself seated near a man who had known her grandfather.

"Your grandfather was a good friend of mine. Many people respected him, for he was never afraid to do what was right. Did he ever tell you about the time...."

Carrie listened and asked questions all afternoon. After stories about her grandfather, they went on to recount tales of long, long ago. She learned of the triumphs and struggles of her people. On the way back, she thought about all she had heard.

Summer

The school year was ending. Carrie would soon leave to spend the summer with her grandmother. But right now, everyone was excited about the big celebration, the powwow. They had practiced traditional dances, gotten ready for the drum contest, sewn clothing, and prepared food. Finally, the day came. The Grand Entry, which would begin the powwow, was about to begin. Carrie wore her beautiful jingle dress, which she had helped make. All around her were the stunning colors and patterns of other native clothing. One child carried the American flag and another carried the staff of the Lakota nation.

The sun was shining and the air was warm, but Carrie shivered a little with excitement and nervousness before the dance. Still, she knew she could do this. Carrie had been generous during the school year with her friends and in her work on the powwow. She felt great respect for the culture she was celebrating right now. Perhaps, she thought, she was gaining wisdom, too, by being courageous, generous, and respectful. Then she would have completed the Circle of Courage. She must work on this all her life; it would make her ancestors proud. And Jesus, too. She said a little prayer of thanksgiving and danced into the circle.

Contentment on the Mountain

A Story from Morocco

DIRECTIONS: After reading this story, have the learners make a list of objects they own that are not absolutely necessary. Challenge them to think about how they could live creatively and well if the list were cut in half. Have them then go over this list to see what they could most easily go without.

INTRODUCTION: This story, which takes place in Morocco, will challenge us as to how we choose to live our own lives. It is based on a real circumstance.

Jakob was enjoying the challenge of threading his way through the Rif Mountains in northern Morocco. The young German man had some time off from his job and wanted to spend it in an adventure. He had chosen this site because he wanted to see how people lived in a very remote area. Jakob was used to hiking in Germany and was prepared to rough it for a few days.

His guide, Oumar, moved at an easy pace on the winding, remote road. Hours had passed since they had seen a car. Pausing from time to time, they admired the beauty of the silent, pine-topped peaks. Jakob inhaled the silence as one takes in a deep breath.

They were headed for the home of a Berber family. Occasionally, the family took in hikers like Jakob, with the arrangements made by Oumar. Such visits supplemented their income and, thought Jakob, brought a bit of the outside world to this secluded area.

The two men arrived at the farm of the host family, and Jakob found that it was indeed remote. He had walked through miles of forested hills, but just how far they were from the nearest town was not as obvious to him until he saw the houses and gardens perched alone in the clearing. A few chickens and eight small children greeted them first. The children, bright-eyed and excited, were glad to see Oumar. He spoke to them in Arabic and the oldest child ran into one of the two houses. She led out several adults who greeted Jakob. They discovered they had one language in common: Spanish. That would make the visit easier. Oumar promised to be back in three days, then left.

The family included an older couple, their two sons and their wives, and the children. Jakob found them to be welcoming, quiet, and polite. A clean guest room reserved for travelers was ready for him. One of the little boys followed him to his room. The boy seemed anxious to show Jakob something, so Jakob went with him. The child led him to a goat pen, where two newborn kids were with their mother. The little boy entered the pen and gently stroked the large goat, then the kids. He smiled up at Jakob, eyes shining. Soon, however, the boy was called away. "Time to pray," he told Jakob.

Jakob nodded. He knew that his host family was Muslim and wondered if they would pray the ritual five times a day. He sat near the house, and listened to the murmur of prayerful voices. As he gazed at the glory of the mountains, he said his own prayers.

After the afternoon prayers, Jakob took part in the family's life. He helped the children feed the chickens and learned to milk a goat. He also offered to work in the vegetable garden. The women shooed him away, saying he was a guest. But they were open to his questions about their dome-shaped clay oven that stood outside, and he enjoyed a piece of hot bread from it.

Jakob was thirsty and was offered a cup of water. But he was uncomfortable about drinking it, knowing that one of the women had probably walked a long way to get the family's daily water supply. In hesitant Spanish, he tried to explain.

The woman smiled and pushed the cup back to him, assuring him in Spanish that they had plenty of water. She pointed to the roof of one of the houses, and Jakob was startled to see some very unexpected objects there. He had been so busy enjoying the view that he had not noticed the roof. The mother laughed and instructed one of the little girls. The child skipped away and returned with the grandfather, who seemed delighted to take Jakob onto the roof.

There Jakob saw water tanks, fed by a spring in the mountains. No one had to walk over the hills with heavy cans of water. The roof also had a solar collector. The grandfather showed Jakob how the energy from the sun was stored in large truck batteries.

Jakob was thinking of all the things he used electricity for and wondered how this family used their power. The grandfather pointed to a satellite dish.

"You have a television set?" Jakob asked incredulously.

The grandfather nodded and said, "Do you like *Sesame Street*?"

Jakob roared with laughter. He was laughing at himself and his preconceived ideas about this family. Then he pulled his cell phone out of his pocket and looked at the grandfather. The older man pointed to a certain area higher than the farm. "If you go up there, you can get a signal," he said.

When it grew dark and the trees whispered in the wind, Jakob sat with the family over a meal of couscous and vegetables. "This is delicious!" he complimented the cooks. He found the food very satisfying. As he looked around at the gentle, welcoming family, Jakob felt very content.

Contentment. That was what he was sensing in the people around him. They lived simply, but with dignity and creativity. They were not wealthy, but they had what they needed. Jakob found he liked the feeling very much.

When Oumar returned to lead him down the mountain, Jakob carried with him a piece of goat cheese, some fine memories, and a resolve to find contentment in his own, very different life.

Shades of Blue

A Story from Ecuador

DIRECTIONS: Discuss the role education plays in people's lives. What are the learners' expectations for themselves in terms of education and future jobs? How does this compare with the boy in the story? How does his future compare to children in greatly-impoverished countries who never attend school?

INTRODUCTION: Some children involved in child labor are not exploited or abused. They must work to help their families earn a better income, but the work is not physically harmful to them. However, this work still prevents them from going to school, which in turn makes it difficult to find a better job later on.

Alano got up as usual to eat with his family and do a few chores before leaving for work. He and his sixteen-year-old brother, Lorenzo, set off for their uncle's house. They were part of a five-member team of painters. Mainly they did inside work, and that day they were starting work on a school.

Alano had turned thirteen several months ago. He had left school, then began working about ten hours a day in the adult world. His uncle was a kind man and a good boss. His parents were grateful that their sons had such good jobs. Alano was glad he could contribute to his family's income. And he enjoyed painting.

The work crew reached the school and began bringing in some supplies and ladders. Alano was to start in an empty classroom with his uncle. He spread out the drop cloths and pried open a new can of paint. The paint was wonderfully thick and a rich blue. He was carefully stirring it when his uncle asked him to go back outside to the truck to get some new rollers and clean rags.

Alano stepped into the hallway just as a bell rang. Students were rushing everywhere. He heard laughter, teasing, and complaining. Books were dropped, papers were shuffled, pens were stuffed into pockets. Alano stopped, knowing he would be trying to walk against the crowd if he continued in the same direction. Students noticed him. Some smiled, but he felt out of place here in his work clothes. Less than a year ago he had been a student here, but now that seemed long ago and far away.

The hallway soon cleared and classes began. The murmur of students and the voices of teachers could be heard through the closed doors as Alano passed by. Outside, he quickly found what his uncle needed, but he paused to look at the school building before re-entering. He had been in a fine mood when he left home this morning, but somehow that had changed. He liked painting, yet he felt as if something were missing from his life. With a sigh, he headed back to the job.

Walking All the Way

A Story from Latvia

DIRECTIONS: Try to find someone in your parish or diocese who has experienced a pilgrimage. Invite the person to talk with your students.

INTRODUCTION: For many years the country of Latvia was under Communist rule, and the practice of religion was restricted. Now Latvians are free, and many Catholics express their devotion to Mary, the Mother of God, by joining a pilgrimage. A pilgrimage is a journey to a holy place. Once a year, near the feast of the Assumption, thousands of people from Latvia and other countries walk to the town of Aglona, to a large church called the Assumption of the Blessed Mother Basilica.

Caitlin couldn't believe what she was about to do. She had on her best hiking boots, but that seemed of little comfort.

It all began when her family hosted an exchange student from the country of Latvia. Silvija had lived with Caitlin's family for the school year. The two girls had become close friends, and Caitlin was excited when Silvija's family invited her to come to Latvia when Silvija returned home. She was going to spend the month of August in this eastern European country!

"Do you want to go on a pilgrimage with my family?" Silvija's mother had asked her. "We are going to the town of Aglona, to a big celebration in honor of the Blessed Mother, for her feast on August 15."

The idea sounded good to Caitlin. Her own family was not particularly religious, but she was open to learning more. Besides, everything Silvija and her family had planned for her so far had been fun. Sure, she'd go.

Caitlin had assumed they could go by car or train. It had never occurred to her that people actually walked for three days straight to go somewhere! But that was what she was doing now. She and hundreds of people, with more joining them every day, were walking to Aglona.

Her feet ached, the calves of her legs burned, her hair was stuffed under a baseball cap, and her nose was sunburned. Never had she been so tired. On that first night, she sank wearily and gratefully into her sleeping bag next to Silvija's and slept like a rock.

But during the day, despite her exhaustion, she enjoyed all that was going on around her. People sang, and Caitlin hummed along, as she only spoke English. Silvija pointed out to her that some people were speaking Latvian, some Russian, some Polish, and a few other languages as well. Soon Caitlin was reciting the rosary in English, alongside an old man who was saying it in Polish. Banners with church names fluttered in the breeze, while young children skipped and danced. Some were on their way to celebrate their First Communion at the basilica. Other teens, grandparents, young parents with babies in strollers, couples, and even one woman in a wheelchair pushed by her attentive husband joined the crowd for a while.

By the afternoon of the second day they were walking through a farming area. Families working in their fields stopped and joined the pilgrims for a short part of their journey. Silvija pulled Caitlin with her, heading toward one family that stood by watching, hoes and rakes leaning against the fence. The family joined the singing of the travelers. As the girls approached the mother and a toddler who clung to her, Silvija pulled a rosary out of her pocket and gave it to the woman. The woman smiled and thanked Silvija, kissing the rosary. The little girl reached up for it and the mother let her finger the beads, both admiring its beauty as Caitlin and Silvija rejoined the group.

As they reached a town, Silvija's mother gave Caitlin several rosaries. "To give away," she explained. Caitlin soon saw what she meant. The streets were lined with tables. Behind them stood older women, women who had endured years of restrictions on their religion. They had buckets of cold water and sandwiches for the travelers. Caitlin ate gratefully and understood that these women were cheering on the pilgrims. She gave the rosaries freely and received many smiles she knew she would never forget .

As she lay down in her sleeping bag that night, her feet encased in lotion and soft socks, she thought of this strange but wonderful experience. The voices raised in song, the voices joined in prayer in several languages, the large statues some people carried, the laughter, the sense of unity—all this, she felt, would never leave her. She knew that some people were making this journey in hope of a miracle that they prayed for with faith. Others were making the journey as an act of thanksgiving. Some were here on behalf of others. All around her she sensed joy, even as people grew weary. She experienced, too, what she could only call a deep sense of God in the other pilgrims.

Tomorrow they would reach the basilica by midmorning. There they would pray and celebrate for a few days. After that, they would take a bus back to Silvija's home. Within a week, Caitlin would be on a plane back to the United States. She would have a lot to tell her friends. But how would she ever be able to explain to them what she had shared with the other pilgrims who journeyed to Aglona?

Celebrating Freedom?

A Story from China and the United States

DIRECTIONS: Discuss the irony in this story: Some people, many of them children, lose their lives making something used to celebrate others' freedom.

Discuss the importance of freedom and what it means not to be free. Brainstorm ways the Fourth of July could be celebrated without fireworks.

INTRODUCTION: For years fireworks have been a major part of the celebration of our nation's freedom. Ironically, though, many of these fireworks come from China where they are assembled by families, including children. The work is dangerous, and injuries and death are frequent. The following description asks us to reflect: Are the children in China free?

Reader 1 It is the Fourth of July, a day when the United States celebrates its independence. In New Hampshire, a family gathers to picnic on this hot day. In the evening, after the sun has set, they bring out a box of sparklers. The adults are careful to keep the children safe and everyone enjoys the starry sparks that light up the night.

Reader 2 Many of the fireworks used in the United States are purchased from China. These fireworks are often low-priced because it is children who make them, and they are greatly underpaid, which keeps the costs down.

Reader 1 All evening of July 4, a neighborhood in Michigan is alive with the sounds of bottle rockets, snaps, and other explosive noisemakers, along with children's shouts and laughter and adults' warnings to be careful.

Reader 2 There was a huge explosion in a school in China. Forty-two people were killed, most of them children. The teachers were requiring the children to make fireworks before going home each day. The younger children, those in third and fourth grades, were expected to assemble at least 1,000 fireworks a day. The fifth graders were expected to make ten times that many.

Reader 1 A driveway leading to a home in Arizona is littered with bits of paper and wire from sparklers, spinners, snakes, and bottle rockets. The remains of an exploded Roman candle stick out of the ground. A faint smell from it hovers in the air as people laugh and talk, enjoying the holiday.

Reader 2 In some fireworks factories in China, whole families work. Each family member makes about two dollars a day. The job may include cutting tubes that will hold explosive chemicals and dipping them into red dye. A factory can be extremely hot, and there are usually few windows or fans despite fumes from the dye. Mostly likely, there are no emergency plans or equipment in the factories.

Reader 1 It is late, and the night is heavy with humidity, but family and friends gather on the lakeshore to enjoy the town's fireworks display in Alabama. A little boy sits on his father's lap and asks why there are fireworks and why he sees them in July. "Because today is a special day in our country. We are celebrating that we are a free people. Freedom is very important! The fireworks are a fun way to help us celebrate," the father explained but he is interrupted by the booming sound that always precedes a colorful explosion. They gaze in delight as a huge orange starburst opens up against the dark sky.

Reader 2 In China, one person was killed and thirty-four were injured in a fireworks accident. All were schoolgirls ages eleven, twelve, or thirteen. Also in China, twenty workers were killed in a fireworks factory. Most of them were between the ages of nine and fourteen.

88

The Big Brother

A Story from Vietnam

DIRECTIONS: This story is a beautiful example of respecting the "dignity of the human person." Discuss who is working to show the little girl her dignity and in what ways this is being done.

INTRODUCTION: In Vietnam, education for everyone is a high priority. As the country adopts a market economy, many new schools are being built because forty percent of the population is under the age of twenty-five. Even in the rural areas, children go to school four hours a day, six days a week, and they have plenty of homework. Due to the large number of children, morning sessions are held for some children and afternoon sessions for others. Not long ago, children with disabilities were hidden from community life and not educated. That situation is changing with the help of organizations such as Catholic Relief Services, which has helped train classroom teachers who work with children who have a variety of challenges. This fictional story about a brother and sister who attend school in rural Vietnam is based on a real situation.

1998

In a village in Vietnam, three-year-old Bai looked curiously at his new baby sister, Thuy Tien. No one seemed happy about this baby. Bai placed one of his fingers into the baby's palm. Immediately, she curled her fingers around his. "Why does Me, my mama, keep crying?" he asked his father. "Why do Grandmother and Grandfather keep talking about bad luck?" His father stroked Bai's shiny, straight hair and said, "Thuy Tien is not like most babies. She has something called Down Syndrome. She won't learn and do things like you. It is very bad luck that caused this. And no one else will want that bad luck, so we must keep Thuy Tien home with us, where no one will see her."

Bai wrinkled his forehead and cocked his head, gazing again at the baby. "She looks all right to me," he said solemnly.

His father smiled, but there was sadness in his eyes. "I am sure you will be a good big brother, Bai."

2002

Seven-year-old Bai felt proud. His teacher, Miss Kien, was walking home with him. She said she needed to talk to his mother, Loa.

"You have a little sister, don't you, Bai?" the teacher asked.

Bai nodded. Thuy Tien was four years old now. "But she has something called Down Syndrome, so people don't want to be with her," he explained. "I like being with her. I play with her."

When they came close to the house, Bai could smell what his me was cooking: fried fish, boiled spinach, and roasted peanuts. He called, "Me! My teacher has come to see you!"

Wiping her hands, his mother hurried to politely greet the teacher. Thuy Tien followed, peeking out from behind her mother.

"I came to ask you to send Thuy Tien to school," Miss Kien said. She smiled down at Thuy Tien, who ducked back behind her mother.

"But that is not possible!" Loa said. "You know she has a disability. Children like Thuy Tien don't go to school. She has hardly been out of the house!"

"But Thuy Tien can learn!" Miss Kien insisted. "All the teachers are now trained to work with children who have special challenges. Thuy Tien needs to get an education. More and more children with disabilities are coming to school. There's a boy in Bai's class who is blind, but he is in school and doing very well!"

Bai nodded, but no one seemed to notice.

"Well, I don't know..." Loa said. "The neighbors, the grandparents—they'll worry about this!"

"Many people are changing their minds about

89

what it means to be disabled and what disabled people can accomplish," said Miss Kien. "An education will mean that Thuy Tien can live as full a life as possible! Please consider this, for your child's sake. We would love to have her in our school along with Bai."

Lao nodded. "I will speak with the rest of the family. But I don't know…."

In the quiet of the evening, Lao nodded to Bai. He knew this meant he must play with Thuy Tien so the adults could talk. He hoped they would decide to send her to school, so he listened as much as he could to their conversation. To his surprise it was his grandmother who said, "If it is possible, then why hesitate?" The others were concerned about how the neighbors would feel. Her father didn't really believe Thuy Tien could learn.

Bai played a clapping game with his sister, and began teaching her a song.

2006

It was time for eight-year-old Thuy Tien to arrive home from school. She went in the afternoons, and Bai went during the morning session. It was his job to be home when she came home, for both of their parents worked away from the house. He helped her with her homework until their parents came home. Concerned that she was late, Bai left his own homework behind and looked outside.

Thuy Tien was there, walking slowly and singing at the top of her lungs. Bai chuckled. She was obviously happy with life today. He knew she was excited about learning to read and add numbers. She loved the other children in her class, especially her Circle of Friends. These students were chosen by the teacher to be special helpers and friends to Thuy Tien. One girl helped her with reading, another helped her during exer-

cise classes. She sat with them at lunchtime and laughed with them over silly things. Thuy Tien also loved her teachers. She listened respectfully to what they said and she did what they expected her to do.

Starting school had been a hard change for her at first, but now that she was used to it, it was fine. It seemed to Bai that the hardest thing for his sister was having her routine changed.

She came into the house as usual. They had begun to do homework when there was a knock at the door. Thuy Tien stiffened. Bai answered and found visitors from the teacher-training program. They had come to see how Thuy Tien was doing in school. Bai welcomed them in and turned to his sister. She was gone. He and the visitors could hear her crying in the next room. Bai sighed, apologized, and went to find her.

She was sitting on the floor, rocking herself and quietly crying. She didn't know these people. She hadn't expected any visitors. This wasn't what usually happened after school.

Bai sat down next to her and put his arm around her. "Everything is all right. We have a little change in our day, that's all. The visitors are good people. They just want to know how you are doing in school. Don't you want to tell them how much you love school and how much you are learning?"

Thuy Tien shook her head.

"Well, then, you can just be shy. But I am going to tell them. Take my hand, and let's go see them. You don't have to talk," Bai said.

"Is this important?" she asked.

"Yes—it's about you being in school!"

Thuy Tien gathered her courage and stood up. She reached for her brother's hand, and together they went to greet the visitors.

The Silence of Hunger

A Story from Zambia

DIRECTIONS: In some rural areas of Zambia, the roads are in very poor condition. Name three ways in which this may contribute to food shortages. (Some possible answers: difficulty in getting to markets to sell or buy produce, difficulty in food aid to be transported over the area, inability to get to other resources.)

Many factors cause hunger. Discuss how the following circumstances contribute to it: severe weather, war, transportation, over-dependence on a small variety of crops, national debt and cash crops, bad environmental farming techniques, water shortage, monetary poverty, refugees, epidemics.

Eddy's family was helped in two ways: immediate food and the tools for growing more food when weather conditions improve. Discuss the difference in these kinds of assistance.

INTRODUCTION: In some remote areas of Zambia, families were already struggling with the HIV/AIDS virus. More than twenty percent of the adult population there is infected. A two-year drought then hit those areas. The extreme weather left farmers not only without food to eat, but also without seeds to plant for the next year. The food shortage left many Zambians without the physical strength to plant, and AIDS has left even fewer people to work. Catholic Relief Services has assisted in this complicated crisis. Eddy and Grace's family was one of the many who have benefited from emergency food aid, as well as from the Agriculture Recovery program.

At midday the village was very quiet. Not a chicken clucked or scratched at the dusty earth, nor were any goats bleating nearby. No women were cooking outside their homes, nor could a sign of a cooking fire be seen.

No children played, shouted, sang, or laughed in the streets.

All was silent because the busy chickens and the frisky goats were gone, either eaten or sold months before. The women were in their homes for there was no food to cook. The children were also inside, too weak from lack of food to be playing or singing.

This silence was known as "the silence of hunger."

Eddy and his little sister, Grace, were two of the children with hollow cheeks and thin arms who lay listlessly in their home. Mama hummed a little, trying to keep their minds off of their hunger, but soon she was yawning. She lay down next to Grace and fell asleep.

Eddy watched her sleep. He thought she was the most beautiful mother in the whole world. He knew why she was so tired. She got up long before the sun rose each day and walked for miles to a place where some wild fruit grew. Sometimes she came home with fruit, and they had something to eat. But this was one of the other days, when there was no fruit to be found.

Little Grace curled up next to her mother and was soon asleep. Eddy wandered out of their tiny house. In the distance, he saw two young men carrying a dugout canoe toward the marsh. He followed slowly.

As he got closer, he saw that one of the men was his cousin Walenda. He watched as the men slid the small canoe into the water. A little way out among the reeds, Walenda dove into the water. He came up for air a few times. Eddy kept watching, wondering what he was doing. The next time Walenda surfaced, he held up something in his hand and threw it into the dugout. He did this a few more times, and then let his friend do the diving. Between them, they found about five or six of whatever it was. Eddy peered hard, but he did not recognize it.

When Walenda and his friend emerged from the marsh, they saw Eddy. Walenda smiled at him. "Here, Eddy, a gift for you. Give it to your mama. She'll know what to do with it."

He handed Eddy a soggy root. Mud still clung to it, but Eddy could see it was purple. Walenda's kind smile told him that this gift was food. He thanked his cousin and, carrying the root like a grand prize, he walked back to his house.

Mama awoke when he came in. In the darkness of the hut, she looked curiously at what Eddy held. "Walenda got it from the water. He said it was a gift and you would know what to do with it."

Mama smiled and took the root. "I certainly do! Did you thank Walenda?"

Eddy nodded and watched as Mama sliced and boiled the purple root. "This will fill us up," she said. She did not tell Eddy that she had to be very careful preparing it because, if not done properly, the root might cause them to get sick. Although the root had no nutritional value, at least the empty feeling would go away for a few hours.

The next morning Walenda came shouting, "They've come! The people with the food have come! We can go get our food right now!"

The family hurried out of the house. Walenda was smiling. "I'm going so Grandmother does not have to. Do you want to come with me?"

Mama said, "I'll get my card and the baby."

Inside the house, Mama put Grace onto her back. From her special box where she kept her most important things, she pulled a heavy cardboard card.

"What's that?" Eddy asked.

"Our ration card. I was given this because we need food." She let Eddy look at it. "It has our names on it and lists how much food we can get. Come now."

Eddy followed his mother and cousin as they walked a few miles. This made him very tired, and the hungry feeling grew worse. Then Eddy saw a gathering of people from several villages. This was the food distribution center. Mama and Walenda both joined the line that was forming. Eddy sat in the shade, holding Grace.

He watched as Mama and Walenda showed their ration cards to a woman who checked each one. From there, they walked over to an area where many bags of food were stacked. Eddy had never seen so much food in once place! He rubbed his stomach but he felt happy.

Mama got what was called a "complete ration": rice, beans, and vegetable oil. Walenda got the same. They would have enough for each person in a household to have at least one healthy meal a day. Food in hand, they had their cards stamped.

But that was not all. In another area a woman had garden tools. She and Mama talked for a long time, and then the woman gave Mama seeds as well as tools. Mama was very happy when she joined Walenda and Eddy.

"When the rains come again, I'll be ready to plant! These seeds are for plants that are better able to stand the lack of rain," she said. "I have seeds for cabbage, pumpkins, and carrots! And, I'll be trained in better ways to farm."

As Mama began to organize the food and equipment, a few beans slipped out of a bag and fell to the ground. Eddy immediately squatted down and began picking up each bean. He did not leave a single one on the ground. Food should never be wasted.

As they walked home along the bumpy and dusty road, Grace dozed, and Mama and Walenda carried the bags of food. Eddy carried the seeds and tools. He was very careful with them.

As he walked, he thought of the delicious beans and rice he would eat every day! Once again he rubbed his stomach. Soon he would have energy to run and play! Inside he had a wiggly feeling that was both joy and thankfulness.

La Virgen de Dolores

A Story from Mexico

DIRECTIONS: Many beautiful religious customs from various cultures honor the Mother of God. Have your learners research to learn of three others.

INTRODUCTION: This true story is about a custom in a Mexican town honoring Mary, Jesus' mother, during the days just before Holy Week.

Joy, a young woman from the United States, had lived in Guanajuato long enough to know the marketplace well. On Friday before Holy Week, she noticed there were bundles of purple and white flowers at most stalls. All around her, market-goers cradled bouquets of these flowers as they did their shopping or hurried off to work. The purple and white flowers seemed to be everywhere. Joy inhaled the sweet fragrance and smiled into the lined faces of the people selling them. A few petals fluttered down from a stand, and Joy noticed there was a softness under her feet because of the fallen petals.

After enjoying her time in the market, she headed to the home of her friend Clara. Clara welcomed her as usual and her two little girls, Lili and Lupe, were excited to see Joy. They grabbed her hands, pulling her into the house.

"Joy, I don't think you have ever met my mother, the girls' *abuela*," Clara said. She introduced Joy to a small woman who seemed intrigued by this tall young American who could speak to her in fluent Spanish.

Lili piped up, "You came just in time! We're making the altar now."

It was then that Joy noticed two vases filled with purple and white flowers.

"It's for La Virgen de Dolores," Lupe said.

The Virgin of pain, Joy thought. She looked wonderingly at Clara.

"Next week is the Passion of Our Lord," Clara said. "His mother suffered so! A mother's heart breaks when a child dies. So we think of La Virgen today, who is so sad because her Son will soon suffer and die."

Joy watched with fascination as Clara created an altar with her mother and daughters. On a table, they first laid a white cloth, then placed a smaller purple one on top of that. "Purple, for sorrow," Clara explained.

The table stood in front of a window, and a purple cloth was hung like a curtain. From the curtain rod, Abuela hung a painting of the Mother of Jesus, pictured with tears streaming down her cheeks.

Lili and Lupe added the flowers, and Clara set many candles on the altar. Then together, they artistically arranged oranges, pineapples, and bananas. Where the white cloth fell in soft folds on the floor, Abuela placed more fruit there.

Green garlands hung from the ceiling. Clara climbed onto a chair to tie more bananas and oranges from the garlands. Joy helped with this task but was soon on the floor with the girls, cutting delicate shapes out of purple tissue paper. These were added to the altar as well.

They stood back to admire their handiwork as Clara sent Lupe for some matches. Then Clara suggested that they each light one candle. "Think of a special person when you light your candle, one whom you want to remember in prayer. In your heart, ask la Virgen to take extra special care of that person."

They became so quiet that the striking of the match seemed loud to Joy. Good rituals bring all the senses to attention, and the sound of that match seemed to begin the experience. Abuela stepped forward first, reaching out to light a candle. She knelt before the altar, deep in prayer. Lili hopped a little on one leg, but that did not matter. The scent of the flowers and fruit hung in the air. Clara and Lupe closed their eyes to pray.

Joy was invited to pray next. She lighted a candle and prayed as the tiny flame seemed to send her prayers to la Virgen. She stepped back and stood next to the abuela as the others each approached the altar. They all continued to pray in silence.

But the group was not silent for long. Soon Lili gave Joy a warm smile and asked, "Can you come back later? Please?"

For the rest of that day, Joy saw more altars to La Virgen de Dolores. In many neighborhoods, she saw other families creating their altars. What surprised her was that there were also altars in front of most of the stores. Often she was offered refreshing drinks of cool fruit water, *agua fresca*, with various flavors: strawberry, jamica, or lemon.

She returned to Clara's home as she had promised. Again grabbing her hands, the little girls led her to a neighbor's house. Lili knocked on the door and when their neighbor opened it, she asked, "¿*Ya lloro la Virgen?*"

Joy silently translated the words. Has the Virgin cried yet?

The neighbor nodded and left the door, returning with three *paletas*, homemade flavored ice. The taste was similar to the delicious drinks Joys had enjoyed during the day.

"These are the Virgen's tears," Lupe said, indicating her paleta.

"And the drinks, the agua fresca—are they her tears too?" Joy asked.

Lili nodded, enjoying her treat. But Lupe said, "Come on, let's go to the next house!"

Walking through the neighborhood, Joy saw more altars and drank more "tears." There was a festive atmosphere all around. And yet, wasn't this about sadness, suffering, and pain?

She looked around her, thinking how she loved the way the people stayed so close to their faith. And, she thought, it was almost time for Easter, where death and resurrection to new life are so closely observed. This celebration, with its theme of tears but joyful celebration, was a taste of the week to come.

AUTHOR'S NOTE: Special thanks to Joyana Jacoby for sharing her experience of a Mexican religious tradition and generously allowing it to be used in this story.

The Immigrant

A Story from the United States

DIRECTIONS: This topic offers much in the way of learning history as well as examining Catholic social teaching in light of a tangible issue. In a Catholic school class studying United States history, the following project can greatly enhance the course. These steps for research combine history, Church teachings, and moral questions. With each step, encourage learners to create visuals that may be used in presentations. Learners in religious education programs may only have time to do one of the steps.

> **Step 1** Help children learn the main reasons for immigration. Learners might research the history of their own families' immigrant background. Consider having learners interview family members, neighbors, parishioners, and so on, to gather immigrant stories. A book of stories might be compiled.

> **Step 2** Research what has been the United States Catholic Church's stance on immigration in history and currently. Discuss how the church in this country is affected by the presence of immigrants.

INTRODUCTION: Immigration has been a part of the United States longer than the U.S. has officially been a country. With the exception of Native Americans, every person living in the United States is an immigrant or a descendent of immigrants. There are times in our history when immigrants were welcomed and times when they were not. Laws involving immigration have actually changed depending on these attitudes. At times when people from other lands are not welcome, illegal immigration is frequent because there are always people who need to immigrate for economic, political, or religious freedom. This complicated issue involves children as well. Based on true incidents, the following story describes one way that children are affected by the controversy of illegal immigration.

Monday Nidia got off the school bus and walked a block to her small house in a Minneapolis neighborhood. As usual, she stopped at Barb's house next door before going home. Barb took care of Nidia's five-year-old brother Mateo and three-year-old sister Terceira, while Mama, Papa, and Tio Martin were at work.

The children hugged Barb, gathered up their artwork to show Mama, and skipped home with Nidia. Mama was just arriving home from her house-cleaning job.

Mama sat down looking tired, then opened her arms. Mateo and Terceira climbed onto her lap

and gave her hugs and kisses. She examined their artwork. She listened carefully as they told her about their day, chatting away happily in Spanish, though they had spoken English with Barb.

Then it was Nidia's turn. Mama put her warm arms around Nidia and hugged her. The girl hugged her back, enjoying her mother's tenderness.

When Mama began preparing dinner, Nidia helped. "How did your teacher like your science report?" Mama asked.

"Great! He said it was the best one! He asked me to read it to the whole class!"

"Nidia, no! Really?" Mama was excited. "Weren't you nervous, having to read in English?"

"No, not at all. I love science, Mama!"

"Yes, I know you do! And you go back and forth between Spanish and English without any problems! I am so proud of you."

Tuesday Mama, Papa, and Tio Martin had a meeting at church in the evening, so Nidia put Mateo and Terceira to bed.

Above the bed that Nidia shared with Terceira hung a photograph of Nidia when she was two years old. In the picture, she was held by her grandmother.

"I miss her," Nidia said, more to herself than to her little sister. "I can't really remember her much, but Mama talks so much about her that I feel I do know her."

"We could visit her," Terceira said.

Nidia shook her head. "No, Papa says we can't."

"Oh," Terceira said, yawning. "Tell me a story, please?"

"Once upon a time, not so long ago, a little girl lived in Mexico with her whole family. They loved being together, but they were very poor. They decided that some of the family would have to leave and go to a country where they could get better jobs. So the little girl left Mexico and most of her family and traveled to the United States with her mama and papa and uncle...."

Terceira was sound asleep.

Wednesday After work, Mama went shopping and came back with groceries for a special dinner for Tio Martin's birthday.

That night, they ate together. Papa told funny stories about the mischief that he and Tio Martin had done when they were little boys in Mexico. Mama laughed till she cried. Nidia pretended to be shocked, and Mateo grinned.

Then the doorbell rang, and in came all their friends. What a wonderful party they had! Terceira danced and everyone clapped. Nidia watched Mama, arm in arm with her good friend Rosemaria, talking about life. Mama looked over and noticed Nidia. She reached out and pulled Nidia closer to her, kissing her on the forehead.

Thursday Mama was preparing dinner while Nidia did her homework. Terceira and Mateo were snapping tiny plastic bricks together to make a house when the doorbell rang. Mateo skipped over to answer the door.

Two men stood at the door and demanded to see Mama. Mateo shrunk back and Mama hurried to the door. Terceira followed her, grabbing Mama's skirt.

"We are from the Immigration and Custom Enforcement. Five years ago you were supposed to return to Mexico. As you have not done so, we are here to arrest you," one man said.

Instantly, Nidia was on her feet and at her mother's side.

Frightened, her mother spoke to the men in Spanish, but one pulled handcuffs out of his pocket and quickly put them on Mama. They started to pull her toward the door.

Mateo began sobbing and shouting, "Don't take my mama! Don't take her away!"

Terceira clung to her mother's skirt and started to scream. She did not cry but gave a shriek of intense fear.

"Please, sirs," Nidia said in her most perfect English, "there must be some mistake. My mother is not a criminal!"

"Anyone who defies a deportation order is a criminal," one of the men said and pulled Mama forward.

"Criminals are bad guys like you!" shouted Mateo, but the men ignored him.

"Please!" Mama said, struggling in her panic to remember English. "Please, I can't leave my children!"

"Please let her stay," Nidia shouted above Terceira's hysterical screaming. "There must be a way to work this out!"

But the men grabbed Mama roughly and forced her out the door, causing Terceira to let go of the skirt dress and fall down.

"Bad criminals!" Mateo shouted, his face puffy from crying.

Nidia picked up Terceira and pulled Mateo close to her. The three stood in the doorway as the men put Mama into an unmarked car. She turned to look at her children, her eyes fearful, but she made kissing movements with her mouth. Nidia's heart lurched when she realized Mama couldn't use her hand to "blow" the kisses to them because she was handcuffed.

The car pulled away.

Mateo turned frantically to Nidia. "Call the police! They can't take Mama away!"

"I think they are a kind of police," Nidia said. "I'll try to call Papa or Tio Martin at work."

Terceira would not stop screaming.

Two weeks later Nidia came home from school as usual. She was tired. Every night now, Terceira woke Nidia by crying out in her sleep.

She stopped off at Barb's house. Mateo and Terceira were subdued. Mateo refused to take home his artwork. "Mama can't see it," he said.

They clung to Barb in a long hug, then walked home without speaking. Nidia unlocked the door, and they went into the silent house to wait for Papa and Tio Martin. Maybe they'd get news of Mama soon.

The Gift of Song

A Story from Kenya

DIRECTIONS: Help learners compare their experience of Sunday Mass with that in the story. How do they experience a sense of praising God? How do they participate in the gathering of a community?

INTRODUCTION: "The Gift of Song" is based on the experiences of some Americans who were privileged to celebrate Mass with a community in Kenya.

Maria was always singing. She sang as she milked the goats. She sang as she walked to school.

But then, her family was always singing. Her grandmother sang as she cooked. Her older sister sang as she washed the family's clothing. Her father sang as he walked to work. Her brothers sang as they brought in the goats. Theresa, her little sister, sang as she played alongside their mother, who sang as she gardened.

And it wasn't just Maria's family. Her neighbors, cousins, aunts, uncles, school friends, and teachers sang each day, too. It was part of who they were.

Maria loved to sing and to dance, too, but today she was especially excited. On Sunday, after her family reached the church, she would participate in the opening procession of the Mass. She and nine other girls had created and practiced this song and the dance they did with it. Today was the first time they would use it.

She would also dance as part of the Eucharistic prayer, along with boys and girls of many ages. Her brother David and little Theresa would join in as well.

She was excited, but not because this was a performance for the others who would come to church. The children's music was not meant for entertaining them but for leading them into prayer. The children's dancing and singing were a gift to God. Through this, they showed God their love. They praised God for being amazing and so very loving. And, this was their way of thanking God for all they had received.

Maria washed her face and hands, and dressed in her blue, tiered skirt. She buttoned her white blouse with the matching blue trim. She helped Theresa get ready. Then the whole family set out for the church. David carried the basket with their meal for after Mass.

The family talked—and sang—as they walked several miles down the rutted red road. It was hot and dusty and the wind stirred the dry grasses along the way. Here and there a grazing goat looked up at them with mild curiosity.

Finally, the church was in sight. Maria hurried over to her friends, each of them dressed in a blue skirt and white blouse.

When Mass was about to begin, the altar boys lined up first. Maria's brother Peter carried the cross. The girls lined up behind them and began to sing the song they had practiced.

The words came easily to Maria, and so did the movement. One step forward, three steps back, one step forward, turn to one side, turn to the other, her arms and legs moving exactly with the others. The steps back meant the procession moved slowly. The girls had planned it that way, so there would be more time for the joyous beginning of the Mass.

Maria's voice rose in song, blending with the others. The altar boys sang, and so did the priest at the end of the procession. Maria's song was joined by her parents, her grandmother, aunts, uncles, cousins, shopkeepers, farmers, teachers, and friends. The music filled the church and spilled out the open door and windows.

Alleluia! We are here to praise you, our loving God! We are here to thank you! Our celebration begins as we sing our love to you! Alleluia!

Part Two

Introducing Catholic Social Teaching

Those that lead the many to justice shall be like the stars forever.
• Daniel 12:3

Christians have a long history of social justice. It is grounded in the Hebrew Scriptures, when prophets such as Isaiah and Micah called God's people to live lives of justice, compassion, and peace. Jesus' call for justice and solidarity and his compassion for those who suffered became a worldwide religion. For two thousand years, Christianity has challenged Jesus' followers to live as he lived. Though there have been failures, loving, merciful, and just Christians have exemplified Christ's love.

In the early twentieth century, rapidly changing social conditions challenged Christians yet again. Popes, bishops, and councils worked to produce a body of social teachings. Through prayer and reflection, they have given us a more explicit language and detailed doctrine than was stated in earlier centuries. These wise teachings are a faith- and Scripture-based response to changing social, economic, and political conditions.

Often these doctrines are summed up in seven principles, though they are also listed in other ways. The seven principles are very helpful in introducing young people to this rich tradition of Catholic social teaching. Below, you will find each listed with definitions written for learners ages ten to thirteen.

The Dignity of the Human Person God made us. What an extraordinary work of art we are! No matter who we are, what we own, what we look like, or who our friends are, we are incredible. We must treat all other persons with respect and fairness, upholding their dignity for God made them as well.

We Are Called to Live in Family and Community Jesus knows that people need other people. None of us can ever live in complete isolation. We all need our families, friends, and neighbors. Jesus tells us to help them, too.

Rights and Responsibilities All of God's people should have food, work, clothes, a home, school, and medical care. These are "rights" and every single person on earth must have them. But many persons do not. Jesus wants those who do have access to these rights to help others obtain them. It is a "responsibility" to see that others' rights are upheld.

We Are Called to Stewardship The earth and all life on it is God's creation. God calls us to be stewards of this great gift. A steward is a manager, not an owner. Each of us has an obligation to manage the earth and its resources in a morally responsible way, because poor management leads to great suffering. This means choosing practices that will conserve our natural resources. It also involves making good use of our personal talents, taking care of our own health, and using our personal property carefully.

An Option for the Poor and Vulnerable All people must have food, water, work, housing, school, and medical care. Those who do not are "poor." People who are more likely than others to be abused, neglected, or cheated are "vulnerable." Our Church teaches that these sisters and brothers of ours must be treated with respect and care and given what they need. Persons who are not poor must share what they have with those who are. Those who are strong and safe are to work to help others become less vulnerable.

The Dignity and Rights of Workers Through our work, we earn what we need to live. Work can also be an opportunity to use the talents God gives us. In fact, in this way we work with God to create our world. Because work is so important on many levels, it is vital that in every job, each worker has safe conditions, reasonable hours, and a fair wage.

Solidarity The world's peoples are interdependent. That means we rely on each other for almost all of our bodily and social needs. Our languages, medical knowledge, and art are just a few examples of how humans have always worked together. Even though huge differences exist among us, we are still one family, the family of God. This means we should view our family not as just our immediate relatives, nor just our neighborhood, or even just our country. Our family includes all the people in the world. As a family, we not only tolerate differences but appreciate them. As a family, we must care about the well-being of each other, making sure other family members have what they need and are being treated fairly.

Help your learners become well acquainted with these principles. Make copies of the above information for them to keep in their desks or to hang on a bedroom wall. Also, make posters of each principle (or have learners create them) and hang them where they can be read daily. Discuss what the principles mean. Regularly ask for examples of a principle in practice or of one being violated. Relate current events to these principles. Talk about how these can be carried out in the home or classroom.

In short, help children become so familiar and comfortable with Catholic social teachings that they begin to see all of their life experiences through the lens of these teachings.

Using the Stories with Catholic Social Teaching

Reading the stories in Part One starts developing a consciousness of social justice. However, there are ways to use the stories to specifically teach Catholic social teachings. Young people must see themselves in these teachings, for they are for everyone. The principles will also help them identify with others whose lives are very different but whose basic needs are the same. Start with the principles that students readily understand, such as **We are called to live in family and community**. Then read "A Garden of Hope," "The Way It Used to Be," "A Locked Door at Journey's End," "Journal of an Amish Girl," and "Christmas in January." These stories may reinforce what young people already know about what they receive from family, thus putting themselves in the context of the social teachings.

Once they can identify with the story characters, try a variety of techniques to explore principles.

- Choose a basic need and discuss what it would mean to lack it. For food, read "Tiny Knots and Heavy Chains," "Just before Dawn," "A Small Act of Friendship," "One Thousand Bricks a Day," "The Runaway," and "Worth the Wait." (See the Index for more stories listed by topic.) Discuss the various causes of the different characters' hunger. Ask yourself how hunger would affect how you function.

- Choose a basic need that can be studied locally, such as shelter. Read "The Way It Used to Be," "The Runaway," "A Place to Sleep," and "Resurrection in Cape Town." List reasons for the inadequate shelter. Research homelessness in your own community (numbers of individuals and families, where the shelters are, if there are adequate facilities, etc.).

- Choose a specific principle and read stories that relate to that principle. The **dignity and rights of workers** can be studied through "Tiny Knots and Heavy Chains," "A Garden of Hope," "Hanging On," "Another Day like Yesterday," "Journal of an Amish Girl," "The Criminal," and "Shades of Blue." This variety of work-related stories offers many perspectives. Which jobs give and which take away the worker's dignity? Discuss child labor and how it violates several Catholic social teachings. (See the definition of child labor in Part Three; for a complete list of which stories relate to each principle, see the Index.)

- Dissect a story, exploring the different ways people fulfill the principles. Read "The Runaway," then find three ways in which Catholic social teachings are reflected in the actions of the adults who are helping Tyrone; read "A Prayer in Two Voices" and ask how Father Mike is giving the children **an option for the poor and vunerable** and stands in **solidarity** with them; read "The Train Platform School," then research the subjects of train platform schools in India and founder Indergit Khurana. List the ways in which Ms. Khurana's schools are good examples of Catholic social teaching.

Part Three

Learning and Teaching

The moral universe rests upon the breath of schoolchildren.
• Rabbi Yehuda Nisiah

Learning about Hunger

Pray Together

For Catholics, prayer is the most immediate response to issues such as hunger. Make praying about hunger a part of your daily routine with your learners. Prayer to end hunger should be included every day as long as people experience hunger every day.

Introduce the concept of a novena by making one, as a class or a family, for the hungry people of the world. Using a map or globe, choose one particular country to pray for each day. Hunger is so widespread that you can choose any place to pray for and your prayers will never be wasted!

Pray not only for those who are hungry, but also for those who are actively working to alleviate hunger. You may also pray for those who play a part in causing it and for guidance on how to take part in solving this problem.

A suggestion for prayer:

St. Paul tells us, "And God is able to provide you with every blessing in abundance,
 so that by always having enough of everything,
 you may share abundantly in every good work" (2 Corinthians 8:13).
Dear Jesus, you saw the hunger of people when you lived on earth.
You know that today there are still millions of hungry people on earth.
We thank you with full hearts for all that you have given us.
We ask you to fill our hearts again,
 this time with compassion for those
 who suffer from want of food and water.
Fill us with a great desire to help solve the issues that cause injustice
 and to make the world a more just and equal place.
Show us the way to do this. Amen.

Understanding the Issues

What Is Hunger?

A quick discussion of definitions will be helpful for the activities to follow.

All people experience some type of hunger in their lives, but what is serious hunger?

Hunger: a condition when persons do not have enough food to provide them with the nutrients they need to lead an active and healthy life.

Malnutrition: a condition in which persons do not eat enough food or eat unhealthy food, resulting in not receiving the nutrients their bodies need.

Starvation: to suffer or die from a prolonged lack of food.

Food insecurity: having a limited ability to obtain food or being uncertain about getting food; this may be constant, seasonal, or temporary.

Why Are People Hungry?

The following activities will help learners understand the varied reasons for ongoing hunger.

A. Hunger Facts and Stories

Materials

Information posters (have enough to accommodate the ten facts [see below] written in large letters)

A roll of shelf paper

A flip chart or chalk/white board

Ten additional poster boards

Markers, pens

Tape for hanging posters

Ten index cards

Writing paper

Directions

Before meeting with the learners, prepare the information posters with the following ten hunger facts. Hang these where everyone can easily read them.

1. Poverty (being poor) causes hunger.

2. There is enough food in the world to feed everyone. Even where there are famines (a shortage of food in a large area), people can get food *if they can pay for it.*

3. One billion people earn less than one dollar a day.

4. Even in rich countries like the United States, some people suffer from hunger.

5. Many poor countries borrow money from rich countries. This creates large debts. The farmers of the poor countries must then raise food that can be sold to other countries. These are called "cash crops." Coffee and chocolate are examples.

6. When land is used mainly for cash crops, other important foods, such as beans and rice, cannot be grown.

7. Drought (not enough rain) and floods (too much rain) can ruin crops, leaving people with no food.

8. Much farmland is owned by rich people or big companies. They control how the land is used, not the poor people who work for them. The landowners keep most of the money from the crops, so the workers remain poor.

9. The food we have is not always used well. People can eat fish and grains (wheat, oats, rice), but over half of all the grain grown and the fish caught are fed to animals like cows, which become food for people. It is much more expensive to use food that way. Meat may be good for people, but when some people in the world consume an abundance of meat, the result is less food (grain and fish) for people in other countries.

10. War destroys crops and fields.

Directions

On one side of the first index card, write the first fact (above). On the other side, write the first of the following information taken from Stories of Hunger. Then write the second fact and second personal story on the next card and so on, until you have ten different cards.

Stories of Hunger

1. Name: Joseph

   Place: United States

   Reason for hunger: Both of Joseph's parents must work at low-paying jobs. By the end of each month, not enough money is left to buy food.

2. Name: Andrew

   Place: Sudan

   Reason for hunger: A severe drought has destroyed many crops where Andrew lives, so food must be brought in from other places. The food is very expensive, and Andrew's family cannot afford it.

3. Name: Mariella

   Place: Haiti

   Reason for hunger: Mariella is fifteen years old and works in a factory making clothing. Even though she works fourteen hours a day, she only earns eleven cents an hour. With that money, she must pay for her transportation to and from work as well as her food.

4. Name: Michael

   Place: England

   Reason for hunger: Though there is plenty of food in the stores near where Michael lives, he has been unable to find a job, so he has no money to buy food.

5. Name: Yena

   Place: Ghana

   Reason for hunger: Yena's country owes money to wealthy countries. Though her parents are farmers, they must raise products that will be sold to other countries to pay off the debt. They do not have the land or time to raise food for their family.

6. Name: Juan Pedro

   Place: Guatemala

   Reason for hunger: All the land near Juan Pedro's home is used for coffee plants, not for food for his family.

7. Name: Tumaini

   Place: Tanzania

   Reason for hunger: Tumaini's family are good farmers but three years of drought have caused crops to fail, and their milk goats and other animals have died.

8. Name: Luis

   Place: El Salvador

   Reason for hunger: Luis cannot afford to buy land. He farms land that is owned by a large company. He must grow only the food the company wants and cannot use the land to grow food for his family. The company does not pay him enough to buy the food his family needs.

9. Name: Lupita

   Place: Costa Rica

   Reason for hunger: Raising cattle also means raising the grain to feed the animals. In Lupita's country, the meat from the cattle is sold to fast-food restaurants in the United States. Raising the grain and allowing cows to graze takes up so much land in this tiny country that too little food is raised to feed the people.

10. Name: Fatima

    Place: Iraq

    Reason for hunger: Because of years of bad government, other countries refused to do business with Fatima's country, so food became scarce. Then war began, making it even more difficult for stores to get food to sell.

B. Writing Their Own Stories

Directions

Read through the posted facts with the learners. Discuss the facts to make certain learners understand them.

Divide the students into ten small groups. Give each group one index card. Show them that each card corresponds to one of the hunger facts. Explain that in order to understand how these facts affect people, they are to read the other side of their cards.

Give each group pens, markers, paper, and one poster board. The small groups will write a story based on the information on the card. When they have finished creating the story, they can write it in large print on the poster board. They may also choose to draw the characters in their story. These posters can then be displayed in your meeting space along with the facts. Now that they have a more personalized view of hunger, they can move on to research.

C. Research and Discussion

Challenge learners to research particular hunger facts and present their findings to the group. This activity will develop research skills and give students a wider picture of the problems of hunger. It will also give them the experience of preparing information and statements for use in lobbying or requesting action to be taken.

Some topic suggestions:

The effect of warfare on food availability

Statistics on hunger in wealthy countries

When natural disasters (hurricanes, drought, infestations) cause hunger: how is food made available immediately? What are some long-term solutions?

Statistics on hunger in a variety of populations such as:

1. The world's children under the age of five

2. Among indigenous groups in a country that is generally well off

3. A variety of countries, comparing percentages of hunger in the populations

4. How food scarcity affects children's education

Some helpful Web sites are:

www.catholicrelief.org See the section "Get Involved," and visit the "Kids' Site" for hunger facts and newsroom information.

www.povertyusa.org This is part of the American Catholic bishops Web site, Catholic Campaign for Human Development. Besides information about poverty in the U.S., you can click on the "Education Center" and find information, activities, and ways to get involved for different age groups.

www.wfp.org The World Food Program of the United Nations has a good site for research.

www.fao.org This is the site of the Food and Agriculture Organization of the United Nations. See information on World Food Day on page 109.

www.who.int.org This is the World Health Organization Web site.

Send home this reflection suggestion: As a family, take an inventory of the amount of food in your kitchen. How many types and what amount do you have of snacks, beverages, meats, fruit, and vegetables? Then ask yourselves: How well do we use our abundance? Are we grateful for it? Is there an area where we can and should cut down?

D. Take Action

- *Contact congressional representatives* to ask what they are doing to alleviate hunger. The letter can refer to local, state, national, or world hunger. When writing individual letters to their senators and representatives, encourage learners to utilize the research they did on hunger. Also help them find out what their legislators' records on hunger issues have been. Learners may need help in formatting and wording these letters.

- *Have students prepare a list of local hunger organizations.* Arrange to have representatives from these organizations come to speak to your group. Ask about concrete ways young people can get involved.

- *Contact the editor of the diocesan newspaper.* Ask if your learners can write short articles on the different topics about hunger they have researched. If the learners are involved in a hunger organization, they might write about these experiences too.

- *Log on to www.hungersite.org.* Show learners how they can donate food for free simply by visiting this Web site and clicking a button. If you have access to the computer, make a chart to track how many cups of food your group donates in a week, a month, and so on. Have a contest to see how many other people each learner can recruit who will commit to "clicking" every day.

- *Arrange for learners to visit a food pantry or meal center.* Help them prepare questions to ask the staff, such as how many pounds of food are distributed daily, how many families served in a month, and so on.

- *Suggest that learners organize a food drive.* Offer assistance to clarify what must be done, but make certain they take responsibility. For example, if this is to be done at the parish level, they must obtain permission to make announcements at church services and meetings; call in the information so it may be placed in the church's printed announcements; make posters to remind people about the drive; send home information through children in religious education classes; make arrangements as to where the collected food will be taken and how it will get there, etc.

- *World Food Day is a worldwide event held every October 16.* This date recognizes the founding of the United Nations Food and Agriculture Organization (FAO) in 1945. It is designed to increase awareness, understanding, and year-round action to alleviate hunger. See www.fao.org. Consider sponsoring an event or joining a local event.

- *Another possibility is Fight Hunger: Walk the World,* a campaign to end child hunger by 2015. It is led by the United Nations World Food Program and partners. See www.fighthunger.org.

Teaching about Hunger

After the students have read the stories and learned facts about world hunger, challenge them to teach others. In this section are suggestions for learners to set up a workshop or education fair to teach children and adults about the facts and issues related to hunger.

The workshop could be part of a school program, a parish festival, a parish meeting, a neighborhood carnival, and so on. Make certain the learners publicize the workshop and directly contact people so they have a significant turnout for all their work. An adult should help with publicity. However, to make the most of this learning experience, have the learners do as much as possible.

If you are unable to carry out this entire project, that is, hold a fair or workshop, the individual activities themselves are a valuable means for helping your learners become even more aware of the issue and be involved in applying what they have learned.

Always be sensitive that you may be working with people who have experienced real hunger themselves.

A. Create an Educational Environment

Display the posters with the stories and drawings the learners made for "Hunger Facts." Also display world maps and globes showing the continents.

Make a sign that says, "We are all God's people. There are six billion of us! One billion live in extreme poverty. About 2.5 billion live in significant poverty. That means forty percent of God's people are hungry." This sign may be displayed with the "Faces of Hunger" posters.

"Faces of Hunger" posters. To make these, collect pictures of a great variety of people from a wide variety of places in the world. Mission magazines, travel magazines, calendars from organizations such as Catholic Relief Services, as well as some Web sites will be helpful. You may also want to include pictures of people in the school, parish, and so on. Learners may create posters with these pictures and poster board, and add a statement about hunger to each poster. Some suggestions:

- Which of these people deserves to eat?

- Give us this day our daily bread.

- 24,000 people die every day because of hunger.

- Hunger causes tiredness, illness, stunted growth, weakness, brain damage, even death.

- I was hungry and you gave me food. (Matthew 25:35)

- God gives food to the hungry. (Psalm 146:7)

- The earth has enough for man's needs but not for man's greed. (Mahatma Gandhi)

- The day that hunger is eradicated from the earth, there will be the greatest spiritual explosion the world has ever known. Humanity cannot imagine the joy that will burst into the world on the day of that great revolution. (Federico Garcia Lorca)

- Every gun that is made, every warship launched, every rocket fired signifies in the final sense a theft from those who hunger and are not fed, those who are cold and are not clothed. (Dwight D. Eisenhower)

- My heart is moved with pity for the crowd, because they have...nothing to eat. (Mark 8:2)

B. Booths

To encourage people to learn more and ask questions, create booths. These can be made with small tables set up near walls where posters and other items can be hung. Display boards, which can be purchased at craft and office supply stores, also help create well-organized and attention-grabbing backgrounds. The use of colorful cloth is also helpful.

Our Hungry Sisters and Brothers Booth

Choose several countries that struggle with severe hunger issues. Research information on issues that either affect the hunger situation or are affected by it (life span, climate, political struggles, geography, employment circumstances, history). Add positive cultural aspects such as contributions to music, science, literature, and crafts.

Then set up small displays or booths for each country, with posters and handouts based on the research. Researchers should be present at their displays to talk with others about the country. Create and print quizzes for participants. Here is an example for one on Tanzania.

Fill in the blanks

1. _____, in Tanzania, is the highest mountain in Africa.

2. _____ is the word for "homestead."

3. Tanzania is the _____ poorest country in the world.

4. A favorite food, ugali, is a thick porridge made from _____, which is also called maize.

5. Most Tanzanians are farmers and most farmers there still use _____ because they have no tractors.

6. Most of the roads in Tanzania are not _____.

7. One in _____ children in Tanzania die before the age of five.

8. _____ is a favorite game in Tanzania.

9. Children make toys out of corn _____ and _____.

10. A _____ is a beautifully printed cloth.

Word list

soccer	enyang	third	paved	Mount Kilimanjaro	stalks
five	corn	hoes	kanga	cobs	

Answers: 1. Mount Kilimanjaro; 2. enyang; 3. third; 4. corn; 5. hoes; 6. paved; 7. five; 8. soccer; 9. cobs, stalks; 10. kanga

Foods around the World Booth

- Set up information and displays on types of food around the world. This is to teach others about the great variety of foods the earth can produce and also to help raise consciousness about healthy nutrition.

- Try to bring in actual food and have pictures or drawings of foods not available for display.

- Choose a common food, such as rice, and have three or more dishes, featuring that particular food, prepared in very different ways in different cultures, for example, rice cakes; koshari (an Egyptian dish of noodles, tomato sauce, and onions with rice); rice pudding; kim bap (a Korean dish of rice and vegetables rolled in seaweed); and crispy rice cereal.

- Allow people to taste some foods if possible.

- Find and print recipes from other countries to give to people who stop by the booth. Have ethnic cookbooks available for browsing.

- Make a list of countries in different parts of the world and the foods grown and eaten in those countries. For example, offer a list of common foods grown in Uganda: coffee, mango, banana, sunflower, tea, maize, ground nuts, cassava, soy, pumpkin, sweet potato, cabbage, and onion.

"What Does Scripture Say about Hunger?" Booth

With a biblical thesaurus, find references to feeding those who are hungry. List them and have Bibles in the booth so participants may look for the Scripture passages. Some possibilities: Isaiah 58:10; Matthew 25:35–40; Luke 16:19–31; 2 Corinthians 9:8–9; 1 John 3:17–18.

Statistics Booth

Allow older children and adults who love numbers to create graphs. Have plenty of paper, rulers, pencils, graph paper, etc. Also have available statistics on hunger or other information that challenges people to make comparisons, perhaps using an overhead projector. Display maps that indicate where the statistics are from.

One possible project:

Numbers of people at risk for hunger in the nations of the horn of Africa region*

Uganda: 0.5 million

Sudan: 2.9 million

Eritrea: 3.3 million

Ethiopia: 11 million

*statistics from www.hungersite.org

Compare these numbers to statistics you provide from other parts of Africa and countries on the other continents. Show where the greatest need is by comparing a country's total population to the number of people at risk for hunger in that country. Then compare these numbers (population at large to those who are hungry) in a developing nation and a developed nation.

Story Booth for Children: Preschool through Grade 3

Introduce younger children to the topic of hunger by having them illustrate a story that they can take home. It will help them better understand the lives of children who face hunger. The story is set in Tanzania. It would be helpful for children to see photos of housing or food preparations in rural Tanzania before they begin to draw. Look in the public library children's nonfiction section for books on Tanzania.

For booklets, give each child eleven pieces of paper. Each page should be numbered and printed with the words of the story as shown below. Then encourage the children to illustrate the words. Help children place the pages in the correct order, create covers, and staple. Very young children may not be able to actually represent the words by their drawings, but they will still reflect on the story as they draw.

Title: Amos and Beatrice

Page 1: Amos and Beatrice were brother and sister. They lived in Tanzania. They shared a small house with their mother, father, grandmother, and two little brothers.

Page 2: Their father planted potatoes, corn, and pumpkins. He took good care of their banana tree.

Page 3: Their mother cooked corn, making it into a thick cereal called "ugali."

Page 4: Amos hoed the potatoes, corn, and pumpkins. Beatrice milked the cow.

Page 5: The little brothers fed the chickens, and Grandmother gathered the eggs.

Page 6: But one year it did not rain. The corn dried up. The potatoes were small and shriveled. The pumpkin vines withered. The chickens died.

Page 7: The next year, it still did not rain. The goat died. No corn, potatoes, pumpkins, or bananas grew.

Page 8: The family was very hungry.

Page 9: Finally, the rain came. The family could plant again. Maybe someday, they could get chickens again.

Page 10: As Amos and Beatrice ate their ugali, they hoped there would not be another time without rain.

Beans for Dinner Booth: Activity for Age Seven to Adult

Explain that the participants will do a project to help them understand the inequality of food distribution among people in different parts of the world.

Materials for Part 1

Set up a table and supplies so participants can do the three plates/stickers/beans exercise described below. The persons in charge of this display will give clear information and directions.

Paper plates (Each participant receives three paper plates, one labeled Rich Countries, the second labeled Middle Countries, and the third labeled Poor Countries.)

Glue bottles (Each person will need glue, so provide as many bottles as necessary.)

Beans (Each person will need a small container or bag containing twenty uncooked dried beans—larger beans, such as lima or kidney, are best.)

Stickers: Stickers that represent people, such as smiley faces, twenty per person.

Paper: One large sheet with this information:

	Beans	Stickers
Rich	16	3
Middle	3	5
Poor	1	12

Materials for Part 2

Poster board (one piece for each person)

Photos (pictures of people of all ages, races, and from many countries—find these in mission magazines and other publications about various cultures, as well as on the Internet)

Scissors and glue bottles (provide enough for sharing in the group)

Part 1

Explanation

There is plenty of food in the world. However, it is not shared in a fair way. Some countries have lots of food. Other countries don't have enough and people go hungry, get sick, and even die from hunger. Today we are going to do a project to learn how our food is not shared fairly.

Directions

Hand out the materials.

Explanation

You have three plates, some beans, and some stickers. The plate labeled Rich Countries helps us think about countries like our own. The plate with the words Middle Countries is about countries in the world where the people have what they need but not much more. The plate labeled Poor Countries helps us think about places where people are often hungry.

The beans are to help us think about all kinds of food in the world. The stickers are to help us think about the people in the world.

First, let's divide up the stickers to give us an idea of how many people live in these three kinds of countries.

- On your Rich Countries plate, put three stickers. That helps us see that in all the countries of the world, only a small number of countries are rich, so the number of rich people is not large.
- On your Middle Countries plate, put five stickers. There are more countries where people have just what they need than countries that are rich. You can see this because there are more people stickers.
- On your Poor Countries plate, put twelve stickers. Look at your three plates. How many more poor people in the world are there?

Now we will think of the beans as the way our food is divided among all the people of the world.

- Glue sixteen beans on the plate labeled Rich Countries.
- Glue three beans on the plate labeled Middle Countries
- Glue just one bean on the plate labeled Poor Countries.

Look at the plates. Look at the stickers that help us think of all people and the beans that represent all the food. If you live in a rich country, you will have more food than you need. If you live in a middle country, you have just what you need but you must never waste food. If you live in a poor country, you usually don't have enough food and sometimes you don't have any at all.

Part 2

Directions

Offer each person a piece of poster board. Participants can attach the three plates to their poster board. Set out the pictures of people of many cultures, along with the scissors and glue.

Explanation

These pictures show us many of God's people. We know by looking at these plates that many of these people go hungry. Choose some of these pictures to glue onto your poster. You may want to hang this poster in your kitchen as a reminder to pray for people who do not have enough food.

Letter Writing Booth

Prepare a table at which people can write to their representatives regarding hunger issues. You will need paper, pens, envelopes, and the addresses for both senators and representatives. Ask that people write a letter that day expressing their concern about hunger in our country and elsewhere. Below is an explanation for young children wishing to participate. A sample letter for children is also provided. You may want to have copies that can just be signed.

Explanation for younger children

There are many reasons people go hungry in the world. Our country also has hungry people. We must care about all of them. Jesus wants us to help them. One way to help is to write to our senators. They are people we vote for, or choose, to make our laws. If they know that children like you are concerned about hungry children everywhere, they may work to make food available to others. So today, you can take action as a concerned person and write to your senators.

Sample letter

Dear Senators _____ and _____,
I am a child of (city, parish, school). I am lucky because I have enough food to eat. Because I have enough, I am healthy and have energy to learn and play. I have learned that many children in this country and in the world do not have enough food. Please help them. Please write back and tell me how you can help them.
Sincerely,

_____

Encourage people to take their letters and addressed envelopes home to mail, or if possible, provide postage and mail out the letters yourself.

Work to End Hunger Now! Booth

Contact hunger relief programs (such as Mercy Corps, Catholic Relief Services, or Heifer International) and ask for information packets, brochures, videos to borrow, and so on, on their programs to display in this booth. Briefly explain your workshop and tell them you want to offer your guests ways to participate in fighting world hunger. Ask if they have any local representatives who could attend.

Well in advance of this event, find speakers who have had experiences of hunger or who have worked with people who are hungry. Set up and post the times when your speakers will be talking. Call the speakers a few days before the workshop to make certain they are still coming.

C. Education through Music and Drama

Using the Stories of Hunger, write and perform skits. If the workshop is to happen over several hours, have times set for specifics skits and post information regarding topics and times of performances.

Music

Entertain very young children by having a musician play and sing children's songs about food (e.g. "Oats and Beans and Barley Corn," "On Top of Spaghetti," "Apples and Bananas").

Storytelling

Choose a person who is comfortable and enthusiastic about storytelling for the following story which is suitable for a mixed-age audience.

Title: Hundreds of Bugs

Explain to the audience: Do you know what locusts are? They are grasshoppers, big bugs that eat plants. Some years, in some places, there are hundreds of locusts, then thousands, then millions! When that happens, the people are in a lot of trouble because the hungry locusts eat up the gardens and the plants in the fields. This story is about a boy who lived in a country called Senegal. The food was all eaten by locusts. You are going to help me tell the story. Watch me and copy my actions.

> Once there was a little boy. He was happy. His family did not buy food from a store but grew their food outside their house. His family's garden was filled with good things to eat (*rub stomach*). A little farther from the house (*shade eyes with hand*) were the fields and trees, where more good things were growing. Lots of sunshine (*make a circle with arms*), plenty of rain (*have fingers "rain" down*), and helpful bugs (*wiggle fingers to indicate small flying insects*) made the garden grow.
>
> But one terrible day, the sky turned dark. (*look up*)
>
> "Oh, no!" cried the little boy's mother. "Locusts! Hundreds of them!"
>
> (*Invite the audience to learn the chorus*) **Chorus:** Hundreds of bugs! Thousands of bugs! Millions of bugs!
>
> The boy looked up, too. The sky was filled with flying locusts. (*flap arms*)
>
> There were (*invite audience to join*) hundreds of bugs, thousands of bugs, millions of bugs!
>
> The bugs started to land. They landed on vegetables. They landed on fruits. They landed on the trees and in the fields.
>
> (*Audience*) Hundreds of bugs, thousands of bugs, millions of bugs!
>
> And they began to eat. (*Everyone clicks teeth as if chewing*)
>
> They ate the fruit! They ate the vegetables! They ate all the leaves on the trees and all the plants in the fields!
>
> (*Audience*) Hundreds of bugs, thousands of bugs, millions of bugs!

Then the bugs began walking off (*rub hands together*), those hundreds of bugs, thousands of bugs, millions of bugs.

And the little boy and his mother looked around. Nothing was left in the garden, or in the fields, or on the trees. There would be much less food this year (*rub stomach and look sad*) because of the hundreds of bugs, thousands of bugs, millions of bugs.

Let's pray for all the people in our world who are hungry. (*bow head and fold hands in prayer*)

Dear Jesus, everybody needs food. Help all the people who need food. Amen.

Skit

Offer this skit as a way to introduce hunger issues if you are having a food drive and/or a fund-raiser for a hunger action organization. It is written here as if you are launching both. Modify it as needed. You will need about eighteen participants to perform. The skit is about fifteen minutes long. You might use it at a workshop or education fair, but you could also use it in school, after Mass, at a church meeting, etc.

The skit is divided into three parts. When performing it, move immediately from one part to the other without stopping.

For Part 1 you will need: Narrator; Group of Hungry People (four or more); Generous Person; fish (make one large, colorful paper fish); fishing pole

For Part 2 you will need: Four fact groups (For each fact group: Narrator; two people to hold signs; two signs with facts, with words written large enough for the audience to read)

Fact Group 1: Make two signs, each with a fact about hunger in your town or city. For example: "Our food shelf gives out _____ pounds of food each day."

Fact Group 2: Make two signs, each with a fact about hunger in your state. For example, "____ out of _____ children in (state) are very poor."

Fact Group 3: Make two signs, each with a fact about hunger in the United States. For example, "Twelve million American families are hungry" or "Nine million children needed food from food shelves."

Fact Group 4: Make two signs, each with a fact about hunger in the world. For example, "One out of six people in the world is hungry" or "24,000 people die each day because of hunger."

For Part 3, you will need: Narrator; two Food Distribution People; World People (ten people for Group A, three for Group B, and two for Group C); signs (one country per sign: India, Mongolia, Tanzania, Kenya, Mali, Angola, Sudan, Nigeria, Zambia, Ethiopia, Peru, China, Ukraine, France, and United States; signs must be large enough for the audience to read.); large basket of food (canned and boxed food, eighteen items in all); fish and fishing pole from Part 1.

Title: The Fish and the Fishing Pole

Part 1: The Proverb

Narrator (*addressing audience*) Hello. I have a few questions for you. Please raise your hand if your answer is yes.

How many of you had the chance to eat breakfast this morning?

Do you plan to eat lunch today?

Do you expect to eat dinner later?

Do you expect to eat tomorrow and the next day?

This story is about some people who did not expect to eat every day.

(*Enter Group of Hungry People.*)

Once upon a time, there were some hungry people.

(*Enter Generous Person holding fish.*)

A generous person, who had all the food she needed, noticed the hungry people. "I must give them something to eat! I have everything I need. I'll share from what I have," she said, and gave them the fish.

The people were delighted and went off to eat their meal.

(*Group exits, putting fish down on the side. Generous Person goes off to the other side.*)

But the next day, they were hungry again.

(*Group and Generous Person reenter, move to center.*)

The generous person saw them again, and thought, "They will be hungry every day unless I share with them something to help them get food for themselves!"

(*Generous Person exits, then returns with fishing pole.*)

She went home, and returned with a fishing pole. She gave it to the hungry people, who were even more delighted. Now they could provide food for themselves. They did not have to be hungry anymore.

(*All exit.*)

Part 2: The Facts

(*Enter Fact Group One. Narrator stands in the middle, Sign Holders flank Narrator and raise their signs as Narrator says the fact on the sign.*)

Narrator   Did you know there are hungry people in (*your town*)? (*Sign Holders lift up signs for the audience to see as Narrator reads each fact aloud. Pause a few seconds for audience to absorb facts.*)

(*Exit Fact Group One. Enter Fact Group Two.*)

Narrator   Did you know that there are hungry people in (*your state*)? (*actions of Group One are repeated with the facts regarding your state*)

(*Exit Fact Group Two. Enter Fact Group Three.*)

Narrator   Did you know that there are hungry people in the United States? (*repeat actions using the national statistics*)

(*Exit Fact Group Three. Enter Fact Group Four.*)

Narrator   There are hungry people throughout the world. (*repeat actions using the international statistics*)

(*Exit Group Four.*)

Part 3: Population and Food Distribution

(*Enter Food Distribution People with basket of food. They place the basket in the center and exit.*)

(*Enter Narrator and World People, each carrying cards with the country names. The cards should be facing inward, so the audience cannot read them. Each person knows which group he or she belongs to and moves into that group when Narrator indicates.*)

Narrator   (*stepping forward*) Imagine with me that this group of people is all the people in the world. In Group A, we have the countries where people are often hungry, or even dying of hunger.

(*The ten people in Group A move together and each raises the country card as the name is called.*)

Narrator   Some of these countries are India, Mongolia, Tanzania, Kenya, Mali, Angola, Sudan, Nigeria, Zambia, and Ethiopia. (*pause for a few seconds*) In Group B, we have the countries where people have just enough food, but nothing extra.

(*The three people in Group B move together and each raises the country card as the name is called.*)

Narrator   They are countries such as Peru, China, and the Ukraine. (*pause for a moment, then gesture to Group A*) Notice how much larger the group of very poor people is. In Group C, we have countries where many of the people have more than enough food, though there are hungry people there, too.

(The two people in Group C move together and raise their cards.)

Narrator   These are countries like France and the United States. Now we will watch as the world's food is divided up among these three groups.

(The Food Distributor People enter and go to the basket. One person takes one can of food from the basket and places it in front of Group A. The second person takes two cans of food and places it in front of Group B. Together, they carry the basket in front of Group C and place the remaining food in front of group C. They return the now empty basket to the center, then exit. They return, one carrying the fish, the other the fishing pole.)

Narrator   You can see the great difference. We want to do something about this and we hope you will work with us. We want to help people get food right away (*motions to fish*). Please bring in cans of food for _____. (*add one of the facts used earlier, such as how many pounds of food are distributed by a local food shelf*) Then we want to help in the way the fishing pole helps. (*go on to explain the organization or project you are raising money for*)

Entire cast   (*in unison*) If we work together, we can make a big difference in the world! Thank you!

Learning about Child Labor

Introduction for Adults

Child labor is a silent tragedy of tremendous proportions. Though it occurs in the United States, most people do not witness it here because it is hidden. It is an even greater problem in impoverished countries, where some of it is hidden also, although much of it is obvious. As with most issues that result in human suffering, child labor is complicated. It is also painful to explore. However, neither of those realities should keep people from becoming informed. That is always the first step toward solving a problem.

In this section, you will find information and activities to help learners study this issue which involves their peers. Following the activities are suggestions for learners to put on an education fair for others. Encourage them to use these ideas, to adapt them to their own plans, and also to create entirely new ideas.

A special note: The issue of child soldiers has been touched on in "A Chorus of War," but is not dealt with in this section. Child sexual exploitation has not been covered in this book in any way. Both subjects unfortunately are very important as millions of children are involved. Those who survive suffer greatly all their lives. Information on these topics is not difficult to find but is truly disturbing. Some people may choose not to expose their own children to these topics, at least, not in a group. Please keep in mind, however, that what are challenging issues for us are daily experiences for these children. Please pray regularly for them.

Pray Together

In working with young people on issues that are as difficult and challenging as child labor, always begin with prayer. We cannot accomplish anything without God's help. Ask for God's guidance to show children that prayer is the first step. If possible, have photographs of children involved in child labor in your prayer space.

Prayer suggestion

Reading (based on Matthew 25:35–40)
Jesus was teaching one day. He said, "You will be blessed by my Father. He will say, 'When I was hungry, you gave me food, thirsty and you gave me drink, a stranger and you welcomed me.' But some people will ask, 'When did we help you?' And my Father will answer, 'Amen, I say to you, whatever you did for one of these brothers or sisters of mine, you did for me.'"

Prayer

Dear Jesus, you teach us that when we help each other, we are helping you. Today we will work together to learn about child labor. We know that the children who are being mistreated are our sisters and brothers. They are God's children, just as we are. Help us see you in each other and in the children we learn about today. Please guide us so we can do your work in the world. Amen.

Understanding the Issues

The section "Information on Child Labor" is provided so learners can more quickly understand the basics of this problem. It is arranged so they can easily use it to create posters, information packets, and so on.

A. Explore the Child Labor Photography Project
(www.childlaborphotoproject.org)

Eleven talented photographers traveled around the world, taking pictures to help educate others on the complex issues that lead to child labor. They also introduce us to the real children and families affected by this issue. The Web site contains photos that best exemplify the expression, "A picture is worth a thousand words."

B. Posters with Information

Consider having learners make posters with these facts. Writing or typing it, creating visual art to accompany it, and having it displayed so they can read the facts often gives them a better opportunity to understand the information.

Information on Child Labor

What is child labor? What is child work?

Child labor: Generally, child labor is work that is especially hard, exhausting, and dangerous; employs children under the age of fifteen; hurts their physical, emotional, intellectual, social, or spiritual growth; keeps them from getting an education; involves long hours of work on a regular basis; does not allow time for play or adequate sleep; may take them away from their families.

Child work: Child work does not harm children in any way. It does not keep them from going to school, nor does it forcibly take them from their families. There are many kinds of work children do, such as shoveling a sidewalk, making a bed, babysitting at an appropriate age, cleaning a kitchen after a meal, taking care of pets, etc. These jobs teach children skills and responsibility.

Why Child Labor Exists

Simply put, poverty and greed cause child labor. More specifically, these are some factors:

- Throughout the world, there are parents who have enough money to take care of their children but many others who do not. Sometimes parents are forced to have a child work because the family needs every cent the child can make. They may want their children to go to school, but they are desperate.

- Some of the desperately poor parents are tricked into thinking the work will be a good way for their children to earn a living.

- In some places, a child can be sold like a piece of property. If a parent owes money to another person, the other person can take the child to work to pay off the debt. These children are often taken far from home.

- Some children work with the rest of their family and aren't able to go to school. The work may be dangerous and too difficult for children. Again, because the families are so very poor, they need every family member to help earn money.

- Many countries have laws to protect children from child labor, but the laws are ignored.

- Some children are kidnapped from their families and taken to places of work.

- Certain big companies have discovered that child labor is great for business. They can force children to work long hours seven days a week and pay them very little. The company makes lots of money from the products the children make while spending little money on its workers.

- In some areas of great poverty, there are no schools, so children work. In other areas the schools exist but have few teachers and supplies. Very poor parents cannot see the point in sending their child to a school that offers so little when the child could be earning money.

Some Types of Child Labor

domestic workers

farmers

carpet makers

street sweepers

electricians

metal workers

brick makers

gas station attendants

fruit, candy, water vendors

factory workers making clothing and shoes

factory workers making sports equipment

factory workers making fireworks or matches

garbage recyclers (sifting through piles of rotting garbage to find things to sell)

miners for diamonds

workers on makeshift public transportation

dock workers in the fishing industry

staff in hotels and restaurants

train and train station attendants

The High Cost of Child Labor

The high cost of child labor begins with the lower costs. Employers who use child workers do so because they pay the children very little. Some children are not paid at all. These employers then sell the products the children made to large companies at a great profit. The large companies then sell these products in rich countries. They charge more money than they paid the employers so as to make more money from their work. However, they can still charge less for products made by child laborers than for products made by fairly-paid adult workers. So, customers like you and me are happy because we are buying a less expensive product.

So the costs are low for everyone but the child laborers. They pay a very high price because child labor injures them in body, mind, and spirit.

Child laborers may suffer bodily harm in many ways.

- The poisonous chemicals some children use in their work may cause brain damage or cancer.

- Many of the jobs children do are dangerous in other ways. They may be cut or burned, may break bones or lose hands or feet. They may even be killed.

- Some types of work may prevent children from growing correctly, and this affects them for the rest of their lives.

- Often child laborers are not fed enough. Too little food keeps children from growing well or from being strong enough to fight off sickness. Lack of food makes it harder to think and to work, causing them to have accidents. Not enough food may affect their health permanently.

- Many employers hurt the children by beating and kicking them.

- Child laborers are often not allowed to sleep enough, so they cannot work or think well. Lack of food or lack of sleep may cause them to make mistakes that could hurt or even kill them.

The minds of child laborers may be hurt in these ways.

- Some child laborers are never able to attend school. Some go to school for part of the year, but must stop to do work during certain times, such as harvest time. They then get so far behind in school, it is almost impossible for them to return. Some families of workers travel from place to place to work. As a result, the children attend many different schools for only short periods of time. They find it difficult to make progress in their studies and improve their future.

Children who do not go to school often or not at all do not develop the skills they will need when they are adults. They cannot get good jobs, and so they remain poor. Their own children often become child laborers and are also poor.

- One of humankind's most important abilities is to imagine. We solve many problems with our imaginations. Child laborers are not allowed the time to develop their imaginations.

- In the world, many children receive an excellent education. The child laborers must live in the same world as those who have been able to learn and think well.

The spirit of child laborers may have be hurt in these ways:

- Being treated badly because one is part of a certain group is racism. Racism causes persons to believe they are bad, unworthy, and unlovable. Many children who are laborers are also part of ethnic or racial groups that are mistreated, so these children are treated badly in several ways.

- Friendships are an important part of being a happy, healthy person. Some child laborers are not allowed to have friends. Many never have the chance to learn how to make friends. They may be very lonely.

- Being able to trust people is very important to humans. Children who are beaten and overworked do not trust those who do these things to them. Even if they can leave their work, it will take a long time for them to learn to trust people.

- Child laborers grow up thinking that their worth depends on how much work they can do. They don't understand that they are good and worthy just as they are. They may not learn that they are children of God.

- Child laborers do not have much chance to find joy or delight in their lives.

C. Discussions

To help learners better understand the implications of child labor, use the discussion questions below, which combine facts and stories that address child labor.

What Is Child Labor?

Read or review the following stories: "The Gift" (Dalki); "Hanging On" (the boy); Another Day like Yesterday" (Kontie); and "Tiny Knots and Heavy Chains" (Ramatha).

Read the definition of child labor (page 120). Discuss which of its points are reflected in Dalki's life, the boy's life, and Ramatha's life.

Why Child Labor Exists

Several factors about why child labor exists are found in "Another Day like Yesterday." Encourage learners to write a paragraph about how poverty and greed have affected Kontie's life.

The High Cost of Child Labor

Read or review these stories: "Yellow Dress for Kalimall" (Kalimall); "The Gift" (Dalki); "Tiny Knots and Heavy Chains" (Ramatha); "The Train Platform School" (Rajini); "Hanging On" (the boy); "Another Day like Yesterday" (Kontie); "One Thousand Bricks a Day" (Safel); "Glimpsing a Soul" (Paimon); "Shadows inside the House"(unnamed children); "Shades of Blue" (Alano); and "Celebrating Freedom?" (unnamed children).

List the many ways these characters are physically hurt in their work. Which of these characters have a better chance to learn and develop their minds? Which ones are the most vulnerable spiritually?

D. Take Action

Educate yourself further on these issues. Nothing is ever accomplished if people are unaware of the problem.

Educate others. In the section "Teaching about Child Labor" you will find ideas for hosting an educational fair on child labor.

Learn about and buy Fair Trade products. These companies establish equal and fair partnerships between the farmers and the sellers. For example, if you buy Fair Trade chocolate, you know that the farmers and others who worked to raise the cocoa beans were paid a fair wage and that child laborers were not used to grow the beans. Catholic Relief Services (www.catholicrelief.org) and the Hunger Site (www.hungersite.org) have information on Fair Trade products.

Visit Web sites to learn ways to get involved. The organization Free the Children (www.freethechildren.org) has a fascinating history that is well worth exploring. This international organization was founded in 1995 by Craig Kielburger, who was then twelve years old. Through Free the Children, you will find concrete ways to act. On their Web site, look for books and videos on how to take action on child labor. Listed also are current projects you can work with and additional ideas about how to get involved to make significant change on a global scale.

Teaching about Child Labor

The following is a catalyst for creating an education fair on child labor. As with the education fair on hunger, this event could take place in a school, parish, backyard, park, etc. Encourage the learners to do as much work on this as possible. If you are unable to hold a fair, the individual activities in themselves are valuable as reinforcement or review for your learners.

A. Create an Educational Environment

If the learners have already made posters with the information listed above, use those to begin setting the stage for your education fair. The more colorful and well designed, the more attention the posters will receive.

Create a dramatic and eye-catching display with silhouettes. Using large, colorful poster board, draw the outline of a child's body. Make several of these and cut them out. Just doing this can help learners realize that those in child labor are people similar to themselves. Have them print statistics and information in large letters onto these silhouettes and place them on walls, doors, above water fountains, etc.

Instead of writing facts on the silhouettes, you might display stories. Using the Story Starters (pages 128-130), write fictional stories about children caught in child labor. Type these in a large font and attach them to the silhouettes.

A variation on silhouettes is handprints. Have learners draw many hands of various sizes on colorful paper. Add one fact about child labor onto each hand. Post these hands in several places (doors, mirrors, vending machines, windows, etc.).

For a listing of concise statistics, visit www.freethechildren.org and type in "child labor" under "search."

A poster listing types of child labor may be displayed, but your learners may also be challenged to take this topic much further. In teams, research to find out the estimates of how many children may be involved in each type of work. Children who are intrigued with graphs and charts can create some based on the research. Research one type of work and write a report on it, write a story about it, or paint or draw a picture showing it. These can be read aloud or displayed.

Several children can create murals depicting child labor in various forms. Write prayers for the children involved in child labor and include these with the murals.

Create quizzes about child labor and distribute these to people as they enter the fair. It will be a quick introduction for the guests and draw them to the displays.

Sample Quiz

Match the worker to a brief description of the work.

A) domestic worker   E) worker making sports equipment

B) street vendor   F) farm worker

C) carpet maker   G) fireworks maker

D) worker in clothing factory

1. Sits at a sewing machine in a dark factory, working fifteen hours a day
2. Is in a factory with no windows, dipping tubes into a red dye
3. Sells candy and fruit to travelers by running out into traffic when cars stop for a red light
4. A preschool-aged child in her house is sewing a soccer ball
5. From dawn until bedtime, does laundry, cooking, cleaning, and other housework
6. In doing this work, a child sprays dangerous chemicals onto plants in a field
7. Sits at a loom tying tiny knots all day and evening every day

Answers: A5; B3; C7; D1; E4; F6; G2.

B. Booths

To encourage people to learn more and ask questions, create booths. These can be made with small tables set up near walls where posters and other items can be hung. Display boards, which can be purchased at craft stores, also help create well-organized and attention-getting backgrounds. Consider covering tables with colorful cloth.

Have each booth focus on one type of child labor. Students working in the booths should be particularly well informed about their topics. They must be able to explain a typical day the young workers have, what kind of tools are used, particular hazards, the age of a typical worker, etc.

Suggestions that would work in most booths

- Make bookmarks with statistics on child labor. Laminate these and give them out at the booths.

- An unusual way to display information is make a "lift the flap" game. Using a heavy poster or display board, write facts in different places on the board. Cover the facts with small sheets of adhesive paper that create "flaps."

- Refer to the section on Catholic social teaching (pages 101–02) to see how child labor violates the dignity of people. Make posters or handouts on this so those in the booths can challenge visitors to discuss this with them.

Domestic Servants Booth

Child labor in domestic work is often invisible because the child workers are often kept in the house at all times.

- Make posters listing the kinds of work a domestic worker does. If the work is done without modern conveniences, make it clear what the chores involve.

- List which countries use children as domestic servants.

- Hang a clothesline with clothing. To each piece of clothing, pin a card or paper with the above information.

- For more visuals, place brooms, pails, rags, etc. against the backdrop or wall behind the display.

Diamond Mining Booth

Mining is a hazardous job. For an end product that is very expensive and beautiful, much of the industry keeps adult and child workers in poverty.

- Research and then create posters telling the steps of diamond mining as well as the living conditions of miners.

- Add information about the differences between child workers and child slaves, as some diamond mines enslave children.

- Search on the Internet for photographs showing mines. Use that information to create a small diorama showing a diamond mine.

- Purchase plastic toy rings, such as those used for party favors. To each, attach a tag. On one side, write a fact about child diamond workers. On the other, request prayers for these children. Have the rings displayed near the diorama and offer them to people who stop by the booth.

Clothing Factory Booth

Help children research clothing companies that use child laborers, as well as the conditions under which the children work. You will most likely find information on large companies, names the learners will recognize.

Collect items of clothing made by or similar to those made by the above companies. Hang the items using cloth hangers in the booth and display posters presenting the researched information.

If these companies are being boycotted, have materials on the boycott for people to take home. Look for information on companies who do not use these practices and have that information available as well.

Chocolate Booth

Chocolate is common in most people's lives. Help guests understand how child labor is connected to it and how they can take a stand against child labor and still enjoy chocolate.

Prepare the following information on posters, bookmarks, overhead projector, hand-outs, etc.

The Story behind a Chocolate Bar

Plant and nurture trees. The trees that grow the cocoa beans can only be raised near the equator, in the shade and shelter of much taller trees. They grow to forty or more feet and are very delicate.

Harvesting. Cocoa beans grow inside pods that are the size of small pineapples. The trees cannot be climbed, so when the pods are ripe, they are harvested with machetes attached to long poles. This is dangerous work and done in very hot weather (100 degrees in the shade). The tough pods must be cut open with an ax. The beans are removed and spread out to ferment under banana leaves. They are turned frequently and eventually bagged to be weighed and shipped. See www.cocoatree.org for more detailed information.

Workers. Because the farmers are most often significantly underpaid for their product, they cannot afford to pay the people that work for them. Consequently, many children of cocoa farmers cannot attend school but work alongside their parents in this dangerous and rigorous work. Other farmers may trick and kidnap extremely poor children to work as slaves. Large chocolate companies purchase cocoa beans from many places, not knowing which are produced by children.

- Create eye-catching and hands-on materials to help people understand how child labor is involved in producing chocolate.

- Make papier-mâché cocoa pods (the size of a small pineapple).

- Measure the height of a cocoa tree onto the wall or create one out of construction paper.

- Display a photograph of a machete used to cut the pods down.

- Create posters explaining the process of harvesting cocoa beans, using the information above.

- Make a safe machete out of cardboard and a broom handle. Encourage participants to use this to try and reach the top of the construction paper tree.

- Have a person at the booth that will read aloud, "Another Day like Yesterday."

- This area of child labor offers a clear-cut opportunity for action by concerned people. They can purchase chocolate produced by companies that do not exploit children or their adult workers. This is usually labeled as Fair Trade chocolate.

- Bake cookies and brownies with Fair Trade chocolate. Offer these for sale.

- You may want to charge only enough to cover the costs, but you can consider charging more to raise funds for a program that benefits child laborers. Tell people of your fund-raising goals.

- Serve Fair Trade coffee with the baked goods.

- Get brochures from the supplying companies about Fair Trade chocolate and coffee. Hand these out and display a list of local places that carry these Fair Trade foods.

- Create a coloring sheet on the process of how a chocolate bar is created. This will help the youngest guests at the education fair appreciate the many steps in the making of something as common as a candy bar. They may not be old enough to understand the serious justice issues of chocolate. However, to understand that when they are older, it is helpful for them to begin to see how our food industry is multi-national and very complicated even for something as small and familiar as a candy bar.

- Ask an artistic learner to draw simple, coloring book-style pictures based on the text below, and make copies of each.

Story: The Chocolate Bar

In the country of Brazil, a boy named Sabastiao lives on a farm. His family grows trees called "cacao." These trees grow fruit, or pods, with seeds inside. The seeds are cocoa beans.

Sabastiao, his brother Paulo, and their father cut down the ripe pods. The pods are almost as big as pineapples. They are yellow or orange. It is hard work to cut the pods down. They use a knife with a very long handle to reach the top of the trees.

Then they collect all the pods they have cut down. Sabastiao, Paulo, their sister Elaine, and both parents cut the pods open. They have to use very sharp knives. They scoop out all the cocoa beans.

They spread the beans out on large mats. They stir the beans around so they will dry in the sunshine. Sabastiao and his father put all the dry beans into big bags.

Sabastiao and his father drive the bags to a place where a person weighs the beans, inspects them, and pays Sabastiao's father.

The ship carrying the beans travels to the United States. The bags are taken off the ship and to a factory. Many more people work with the beans. One is a woman named Shirley, who cleans the beans. Jacob heats, or roasts, them.

Miguel and Roberta grind the beans until they become a powder. Janelle, Patrick, and Lois cook the powder with milk, butter, and sugar. The mixture is poured into molds so the candy will be the right shape. Finally, your candy bar is made! But you can't eat it yet because it is still in the factory.

Gary operates the machines that wrap the candy bars. Maria, Elena, and Ralph put the candy bars into boxes. The boxes are loaded onto trucks.

Tom and Robert drive the trucks to stores. At one store, Sara opens the boxes and puts the candy bars on the shelves. Now you can buy and eat the candy bar. Enjoy! And say a prayer for all the people who helped bring you the candy bar.

Prepare a "scavenger hunt" quiz to be handed out at this booth. Using the facts on child labor and Catholic social teaching that will be posted for participants to see, create the quiz. Participants go around to gather answers to the quiz. Those who complete it correctly get a free chocolate—Free Trade, of course!

Brick Makers Booth

Use the story "A Thousand Bricks a Day" to help people understand the daily life of a family of brick makers.
Find a volunteer to do readings of the story at the booth.

Give listeners a handout that lists the times of day mentioned in the story. Ask them to write what they are typically doing at these times in the space provided.

Sample

4 AM   The family wakes. _____

5 AM   Safel and his family walk to a field and begin digging up the clay soil.

_____

10 AM   Safel and his brother and sister carry the newly made, wet bricks to a place to dry and line them up next to drying bricks. _____

At the bottom of this sheet, add: "When you go to bed tonight, please pray for all the exhausted brick-making families across the world."

Use the time theme to create an eye-catching poster for the booth where the storyteller is sitting. Draw a large clock and print the words, "A day in the life of a child brick maker." Next to the clock, list the schedule found in the story.

Bring in several bricks and a cloth bag. Ask adults if they would try carrying the bricks in the bag on their backs or heads. An adult must oversee this.

Video Booth

Locate videos about children in countries where there is great poverty. Call diocesan education offices that may have lending libraries. Check parish libraries, too. Other good sources are Maryknoll (www.maryknoll.org), Free the Children (www.freethechildren.org), and UNICEF (www.unicef.org). Set up a booth with a video or DVD player and have continuous showings.

Newscast Booth

This offers yet another way to give participants information on the injustice of child labor.

Set up a booth to look like a desk for a television newscast.

Have students prepare reports on child labor (statistics, different types, repercussions on children, how to avoid purchasing products made by children under these adverse conditions, etc.).

Learners can dress to look like news anchors and take turns reporting on their findings to their television audience.

Dare to Dream Booth

Create an additional booth entitled "Dare to Dream," placed where guests will meet after they have visited most of the other booths.

Ask participants to ponder this question: What might happen in our world if all child labor were eliminated and all children received a good education, adequate food, clean water, medical care, shelter, and love?

Have an empty notebook for people to write their speculations, hopes, and dreams.

A variation of this is to hang a poster board with the words "Dare to Dream." Invite participants to write their dreams onto pieces of paper with adhesive, and they can stick their ideas onto the poster. Using different colors of paper, the poster will become a rainbow of dreams and hopes.

Have prayer cards at this booth. Learners can write prayers for the children involved in child labor. Create cards with these prayers and laminate them. Ask people to make a commitment to pray for these children. Give them a prayer card as a reminder to pray.

Supply information on Free the Children and other organizations working to end child labor. Be knowledgeable about ways in which people can get involved.

C. Education through Drama

Dramatic readings are an effective and often powerful way to inform people of the challenges others face in their lives. Any of the child labor stories named above can be read at an education fair. Short plays and skits are also good. Below is an assortment of simple dramatizations for an education fair. In addition, these might be used during a class, performed by learners for younger children in a school or other programs, at all-school performances, at a parish event, and so on.

Story Starters

This is a collection of ideas for students to use in any way that inspires them. They could write skits based on them, pantomime them as one person narrates, write stories to be read to others, used for inspiration to create murals, be performed as puppet shows, etc.

Story Starter #1:

On the Fourth of July, as you watch the fireworks light up the sky in sparkling colors, do you ever wonder who makes the fireworks? Fireworks factories in some countries employ children or their families. Each family member may make as little as two dollars a day. Some of the jobs involve cutting tubes that will hold the explosive chemicals, dipping them into red dye, and punching out holes in a tube so the chemicals can be poured into them. The factory can be extremely hot, and there are few windows or fans. Many of the workers, including children, are covered with the red dye, and the fumes from the dye fill the air.

Because these are fireworks, they catch fire easily. A factory can be filled with flames in seconds, and there have been serious fires in some places. Usually, no plan is in place for what workers are to do in an emergency, and no emergency equipment is available.

Story Starter #2

Walking along a street of a busy city, people see a girl, about ten years old, sitting on the ground beside a heavy slab of stone. She wears a long skirt and a blouse, and her eyes are downcast as she works. In her hand is a hammer. She is given old bricks which she places on the stone and smashes with the hammer. The bits of the old brick will be recycled into new bricks. She works from dawn to dusk, but she earns no money. For her work she gets some food and a place to sleep. This girl hopes that someday she can become a teacher, but she cannot even go to school herself.

Story Starter #3

Picture a vehicle called a "tempo." It is like a minivan with no door in the back, and is used as a taxi. Tempo drivers hire young boys to announce stops, collect fares, and to stop anyone who tries to get off without paying.

A boy working on a tempo stands on the back of the van, hanging onto the frame of the open door. The tempo driver makes frequent stops and drives through crowded streets, often swerving to miss other traffic. The boy on the back can easily be thrown off the tempo and run over by other cars. Many tempo workers have broken bones or have been hurt even worse.

When the boy is hanging onto the tempo, he is breathing in gas fumes and black smoke. He works twelve hours a day and makes less than one dollar a day.

Story Starter #4

Imagine a girl living in a big city. She is about eight years old and is a domestic worker. She stays in the house where she works because her employers do not let her go outside. She gets up very early and helps cook breakfast. She cleans the kitchen and carries wet, heavy laundry up the stairs. She must take care of a baby and a four-year-old child. If they make a mess, she is scolded or hit, and must clean it up. She often works all day and into the evening. She never gets to play with other children, nor does she go to school. At night, she sleeps on the floor in the kitchen.

Story Starter #5

A brother and sister are growing up on a tobacco plantation. It is harvest time, and the owner of the plantation demands so much work from their father and mother, it is impossible to finish. The children must help. Harvesting includes many jobs. All of them are exhausting, and some are dangerous.

They have already built the drying sheds for the tobacco leaves, and went into the forest to cut down and haul home long logs to become drying poles. Now they are in the fields. Wherever they are, they must watch out for dangerous snakes. Some days, hour after hour, they pick the large leaves, lug them to the drying sheds, and spend the rest of the day tying them to the poles. Other days they help with the drying, which involves using a fire. Once the leaves are dry, the children must tie them into large bundles. When all the tobacco leaves are out of the fields, the sister and brother spend days burning the tobacco stems. At night their arms and legs ache and they are often hungry.

Story Starter #6

Four boys huddle together against the wind and rain. They are on a platform, about six feet by ten feet. There are no sides to it, and there are a few holes in the floor. The platform is standing in the ocean several miles off shore.

Here they must work, catching small crustaceans called "krill." But in the driving rain, they cannot work. Even on sunny days when they work, they cannot hope for food other than rice and fish. At night, they lay down on the holey wooden platform to sleep. They are not able to go home for months.

Story Starter #7

From where the girl is standing, she can see the mountains in Guatemala, especially the volcano. But mostly she is interested in the mountain closer to her, the mountain of garbage. Along with many other people, she will "mine" this mountain, sifting through rotting vegetables for a few good ones to eat. While vultures swoop above her, she will dig through carcasses of animals to find something like a bowl or a chair or some cans that she can sell. She may even find a toy for her little brother.

Story Starter #8

This boy is one of about one million children in the world who work as miners. Some work above ground, others underground. Many carry loads heavier than they are, while others stand in water for hours. Children crawl through tunnels no wider than their bodies. Other children set explosives. Most breathe in harmful dusts. But this particular boy, who lives in South America, uses mercury to work gold out of rocks. Although mercury is very poisonous, the boy wears no gloves or other protective clothing.

Skits

With a little preparation and a few props, the following skits can be performed for any number of events.

Skit #1: The Gift

Actors

> Reader 1: a narrator
> Dalki: a ten-year-old girl from Pakistan who works in a clothing factory
> Reader 2: a narrator
> Megan: a ten-year-old girl from the United States
> Mom: Megan's mother
> Boss: Dalki's boss

Props

> **For Megan:** sweatshirt with a cartoon character on the front, table, chair, dishes, envelope, a gift wrapped in tissue (the sweatshirt)
> **For Dalki:** fabric pieces in the same color as the sweatshirt, sewing machine or a cardboard box painted to look like a sewing machine, table, chair

Setting

> Two tables with props on opposite sides of each other.

The Gift

(Reader 1 enters and stands near the table with the sewing machine and pieces of cloth. Reader 2 enters and stands near the table with the stacked dishes and gifts.)

Reader 1   This is the story of two girls. Megan lives in the United States and Dalki lives in Pakistan. They have two things in common: they are both ten years old and they both have held a certain yellow (*or whatever color is available*) sweatshirt in their hands.

(Mom enters, sets table with dishes.)

Reader 2 Megan woke up on the morning of her birthday. She was ten years old now! She bounded out of bed and hurried to the kitchen where her mother was making a big breakfast.

(Megan enters, sits at table.)

Mom Happy birthday! Blueberry pancakes for the birthday girl! *(serves Megan)*

Reader 1 That same morning, Dalki was up early. She had to get to her sewing machine in the factory to get in fifteen hours of work that day.

(Dalki enters, sits at table with sewing machine.)

Reader 1 In the noisy factory, she took her place along with other girls. She picked up yellow sweatshirt fabric and began to sew.

Reader 2 There were gifts at Megan's place. She could hardly finish her pancakes because she wanted to open her presents.

Reader 1 Dalki's stomach rumbled. Her head felt a little dizzy because she had not eaten since the night before. Still, she kept sewing, for she feared the man who ran the factory.

(Boss enters, stands some way behind Dalki.)

Reader 1 Dalki worked as fast as she could. For each finished shirt, she was paid five cents. She didn't know the shirts she made sold in stores from more than seventeen dollars. What she did know was that she never had a day off, and after fifteen hours of work each day, she had no time or energy left for fun or school.

Reader 2 Megan's birthday had fallen on a Saturday this year, so she had the whole day to enjoy it. First she opened her gifts.

Megan *(opens envelope while Mom looks on)* It's from Uncle Max! He sent me twenty-five dollars! Now I can buy that purse I've been wanting!

Mom Go ahead and open the present from Grandma.

Reader 1 Dalki had now been at the sewing machine for several hours and her shoulders ached. Her hunger was greater. She blinked her eyes, trying to see better in the dim light. Then her fingers slipped and the machine cut a tiny hole in the fabric.

(Boss comes forward quickly, mimes "slapping" Dalki across her head. Dalki slumps forward. Boss pulls her upright by grabbing the back of her shirt.)

Boss You do that again and you'll get worse, do you hear?

(Dalki nods, shaking. Exit Boss.)

Reader 2 Megan tore open the tissue paper. There was a yellow sweatshirt with one of her favorite cartoon characters.

Megan Awesome! I love it! I'll go call Grandma to thank her.

Mom Good. Tell her we'll meet for lunch after you and I go shopping.

(Mom and Megan exit.)

Reader 1 Dalki went on sewing the yellow fabric, adding the piece that had a face of a cartoon character on it. She had ten more hours to work that day.

(Exit Readers 1 and 2. Dalki continues to work.)

Index

The stories are indexed here by three categories: Catholic social teaching principles, topic, and country.

Catholic Social Teaching

The Dignity of the Human Person

While human dignity is inherent in some way in all the stories, the ones listed here show one person (or a group) recognizing another's dignity, or the negative effect when someone is strongly denied dignity.

We Are Called to Live Life in Family and Community

These stories portray healthy relationships among family and community members.

Rights and Responsibilities

This selection includes stories about people whose rights are denied, or about those who take responsibility to give others their rights.

We Are Called to Stewardship

These stories fall into two categories: stories that show people living with a consciousness that because we are all connected, we must be conscious of others' needs, or stories about weather-induced environmental problems affecting people.

An Option for the Poor and Vulnerable

These are stories of people "going the extra mile" for those who are most disadvantaged.

The Dignity and Rights of Workers

Listed here are two categories: stories that show the ways in which people have dignity in their work, and stories of child labor, an obvious violation of this principle.

Dignity in work

Child Labor

Solidarity

All of the stories are written to help the readers realize a sense of solidarity with others, no matter how different their life circumstances may be. To facilitate this, lead simple discussions after reading the stories on how you would feel if confronted by this story situation, which character seemed the most like you, if you see a solution to any problems, and if you are interested in visiting this place.

Topic

AIDS

Child Labor

Community/Friends

Country